Get A Laugh!

Get A Laugh!

Over 500 Jokes and Anecdotes about Modern Life

Edited by
Joe Claro

Random House
New York

Get A Laugh!: Over 500 Jokes and Anecdotes about Modern Life

This book is available for special purchases in bulk by organizations and institutions, not for resale, at special discounts. Please direct your inquiries to the Random House Special Sales Department, toll-free 888-591-1200 or fax 212-572-4961.

Please address inquiries about electronic licensing of reference products, for use on a network or in software or on CD-ROM, to the Subsidiary Rights Department, Random House Reference & Information Publishing, fax 212-940-7370.

Visit the Random House Information and Publishing Web site:
www.randomwords.com
Typeset and printed in the United States of America.

Library of Congress CIP Data is available.

First Edition
0 9 8 7 6 5 4 3 2
March 2001

ISBN 0-375-70825-1

New York   Toronto   London   Sydney   Auckland

· *Contents* ·

· *Introduction* ·

No matter what claims pet owners make, humans are the only creatures with a sense of humor. And as far as anyone can tell, humor seems to be about as old as—well, humanness. You'll find an appreciation of humor in virtually every ancient text, no matter where in the world it springs from. The *Iliad* and the *Odyssey,* the Upanishad and the Bible, all have their samples of humor, even if they don't begin with "A man walks into a bar. . . ."

In fact, some deep thinker once said that if Adam and Eve were to return to Earth today, the only things they'd recognize would be the jokes.

With that thought in mind, we offer you this modern selection—some brand new jokes, some familiar ones in new clothing, and some that might make Adam and Eve feel right at home in the New Millennium.

And remember that laughter is infectious, and it's your responsibility to pass it on.

■ ■ ■

PART ONE

Y1K to Y2K

▲

As long as we're being Millennium-conscious, we thought some historical groundwork might make for a good beginning. So, for openers, travel back with us to Y1K, the first century of the Old Millennium.

▼

October 1066. Two Norman soldiers relaxing after the Battle of Hastings.

First Soldier: What a battle! What a victory! You know, I have a feeling that someday schoolchildren will read about this battle as one of the turning points in history.

Second Soldier: Maybe. But the books will have to protect the kids from most of the details.

First Soldier: Why?

Second Soldier: Too much Saxon violence.

➜ *A couple of hundred years after the Norman invasion, just about everyone in Britain was*

*speaking English. In 1475 William Caxton
published the first book ever printed in
English. In some of his later books, Caxton
filled out extra pages by adding a joke or two.
Here's a modern version of what just may be
the first joke ever printed in English.*

A widower used all his wiles to get a widow to
marry him. When she finally agreed, one of her
young servant girls spoke to her privately.

"I have heard," said the girl, "that you have
agreed to marry him."

"Yes," her mistress said.

"But mistress," the girl said, "I have heard he is
a dangerous man. They say that he had carnal
knowledge of his wife so often that it was the
cause of her death."

The widow thought about this. A slight smile
grew on her face. Finally she said, "With all the
sorrow in this world, there are worse things than
dying."

→ *All right, so we don't hear any knees being
slapped over that one. Maybe this one, first
published in 1583, will be more to your liking.*

. . .

There came unto Rome a certain gentleman who looked very like Caesar Augustus. The emperor noticed him and demanded of him if his mother had sometimes been to Rome.

"No," said the gentleman, "but my father hath often been."

→ *With just a tiny bit of tinkering, that joke would work as well this year as it did in 1583. And speaking of tinkering, take a look at the next two jokes, with special attention to their dates of publication.*

A minister gave a heartfelt eulogy for the deceased, so effective that it had everyone in tears. Everyone, that is, except one woman sitting in the back of the church.

After the service, the minister approached the woman and said, "Can I ask why you weren't crying before?"

"Certainly," the woman said. "I don't belong to this congregation."

(from a joke book published in 1989)

. . .

A melting sermon being preached in a country
church, all fell a weeping, except a country man,
who being ask'd why he did not weep with the
rest?

"Because," says he, "I am not of this parish."

(from a joke book published in 1697)

→ *So—as you go through this book (or any other
joke book), don't complain about old jokes.
Just about all jokes are old jokes. As a joke
teller, your job is to touch them up, tweak them
a little, reshape them. If you're good at it, your
jokes will sound custom-made for whatever situation you're in.*

→ *Now let's move up through that Old Millennium with some stories that might be true,
some that are very likely to be fictional, and a
handful of funny quotes.*

Back in 1485, ten-year-old Michelangelo Buonarroti spent much of his time hiding from his father.
The old man worked for the government of Flo-

rence, and he expected his son to follow in his footsteps.

Michelangelo, however, wasn't much interested in a spot in the bureaucracy. He saw himself as an artist. His mother was very pleased with his ambition, and she spent much of her time taking the boy's side against her husband.

One day, Signor Buonarroti came home and found his son—as usual—daydreaming on his bed. He went to his wife to complain, and they had one of their standard arguments about the boy's future.

After the usual give-and-take, the father gave up in disgust. Storming from the room, he sputtered, "I don't know how he's ever going to amount to anything if he spends his time lying on his back looking at the ceiling!"

In 1519 soldiers from Spain moved in on Montezuma in search of gold. A squad of soldiers captured one of the Aztec chieftains with the intention of forcing him to tell where the gold could be found.

The Spanish captain said to his interpreter, "Tell him to lead us to the gold or I'll have him put in prison."

The interpreter repeated this in Aztec. The

chieftain said, "I would die before I would tell him."

The interpreter said, "He says he'd rather die than tell you."

Annoyed, the captain said, "Tell him I'll have him tortured."

After the interpreter passed this message on, the chieftain said, "I would die before I would tell him."

"He says he'd rather die than tell you."

Angry, the captain said, "Tell him I'll see to it that he dies a very slow death if he doesn't speak up!"

When the chieftain heard this in Aztec, he said, "All right. The gold is hidden in a small cave just beyond the hill over there."

"What did he say this time?" the captain asked.

Hiding a sly smile, the interpreter said, "He says he'd rather die than tell you."

Money is like muck, not good except it be spread.
                    Francis Bacon (1561–1626)

Late for an important appointment, French philosopher René Descartes sat steaming while the driver of his carriage tried to get his horse to move. Finally, out of patience, Descartes jumped out, stalked to the front of the carriage, and pulled on the reins. The horse bolted and knocked the philosopher to the ground.

A woman who had been watching the incident walked up to the driver of the carriage. "I hope you've learned a lesson from this," she said.

"Lesson?" the driver said. "What lesson?"

"Never put Descartes before the horse."

A friend of Descartes asked if he'd like to go with him to the theater. After thinking it over, Descartes said, "I think not," and he promptly disappeared.

Put your trust in God and keep your powder dry.
                                    Oliver Cromwell's
                                    advice to his soldiers, 1653

Who is rich? He that is content. Who is that? Nobody.
                        Benjamin Franklin (1706–1790)

Canada is useful only to provide me with furs.
                        Madame de Pompadour (1721–1764)

Drinking when we are not thirsty and making love at any time . . .: that is all there is to distinguish us from the other animals.

Pierre-Augustine de Beaumarchais (1732–1799)

Banking establishments are more dangerous than standing armies.

Thomas Jefferson (1743–1826)

I do not want people to be very agreeable, as it saves me the trouble of liking them a great deal.

Jane Austen (1775–1817)

An ugly baby is a very nasty object, and even the prettiest is frightful when undressed.

Queen Victoria (1819–1901)

➜ *And finally, before we plunge into a sea of jokes, an exchange that was supposed to have taken place between two 20th-century icons from the British Isles—George Bernard Shaw and Alfred Hitchcock. If the two of them walked down the street together, they could easily have been mistaken for the number 10.*

Hitchcock: George, anyone looking at you would think there was a famine in England.

Shaw: Alfred, anyone looking at you would think you had caused it.

PART TWO

■ ■ ■

The Way We Live Now

▲

So much for the Millennium That Was. Here's a look at what current life looks like through the sharp lens of the joke tellers.

We've divided a couple of hundred jokes in this section into an alphabetical listing of topics. But don't be fooled by the arbitrary divisions. Most of these jokes can be easily molded to apply to almost any aspect of modern life.

▼

• *Academics* •

Professor Cullen's Tuesday morning literature class was filled with some of the densest students he'd ever been faced with. Most of his Monday nights were sleepless, as he dreaded the prospect of once again trying to simplify concepts for the blank faces that would stare at him the next morning.

During one particularly painful session, Cullen spent nearly an hour explaining and illustrating figures of speech. When he asked if there were any questions, there was a long silence. Finally, a young man in the back row raised his hand.

"Yes?" Cullen said.

The student screwed up his face and said, "Could you put that whole explanation in a nutshell?"

Suppressing his frustration, Cullen sighed and said, "Just get the information into your brain. Then it will be in a nutshell."

. . .

Professor Romano noticed one of his medical students staring out the window during a lecture. Pointing to the x-ray on the computer screen, he said, "This patient has a severe limp because of the unusual shape of the fibula. Mr. Chan, what would you do in this case?"

Startled by the question, the daydreaming student looked at the screen, hesitated, then said, "Why . . . I suppose I'd limp, too."

During the commencement address being given by the new president of the college, Professor Langston leaned over to the woman sitting next to him and whispered, "Can you believe the board could have hired someone so stupid as president?"

The woman's eyes widened, her nostrils flared, and she whispered fiercely, "Do you know who I am?"

"Why, no," Langston said.

"That's my husband up there," she hissed.

After a few seconds of silence, Langston said, "I see. Do you know who I am?"

"Certainly not," she said.

"Good," he said, sliding away and disappearing into another row.

• *Accidents* •

While crossing a busy midtown street against the light, an elderly man was struck by a taxi. A crowd began to form immediately, and the distraught driver climbed out of his cab and yelled, "Please stand back and give him some air. I've already called for an ambulance on my cell phone."

He looked down at the man on the ground and said, "They'll be here in a few minutes. Here, let me put my jacket under your head. Are you comfortable?"

The old man looked up, shrugged, and said, "I make a good living."

The insurance company lawyer was determined to discredit the eyewitness to the accident. "Now, Ms. Gomez," he said, "you say that you actually saw the accident happen."

"Yes, I did."

"And about how far away from the scene would you say you were standing?"

"Sixteen feet, eight inches," Ms. Gomez replied calmly.

The lawyer's eyebrows shot up for the benefit of the jury. "Sixteen feet, eight inches," he repeated. "And just how can you be so sure of that exact distance?"

"I had a tape measure in my pocket and I used it," she said. "Something told me some stupid lawyer was going to ask me that question."

• *Bureaucrats* •

In his dogged attempts to enforce the provisions of the equal employment opportunity laws, a state official wrote to the human resources department of a large company, "Please send us a list of all your employees, broken down by sex."

The head of the department replied, "We keep careful records of the medical history of all our employees. As far as we can tell, none of them have been broken down by sex."

Trying to get some information about her Social Security account, Shepard talked on the phone first with a clerk, then a claims representative, then a supervisor, and finally a district manager. After all those phone calls, she still knew no more than when she had begun.

In desperation, she e-mailed her congressman to see if he could get something done. The reply was a form letter that said, "Thank you for your letter of support. I encourage you to visit our nation's Capitol to see your government in action."

Furious, she replied, "In action? In action! First, someone's going to have to tell me if that's two words or one."

• *Butchers* •

The butcher looked out the store window and sighed. "Here comes Mr. Crabapple," he said to his new assistant. "In 40 years in this business, Crabapple is the nastiest customer I've ever had."

"What do you mean?" the assistant asked.

"Just watch," the butcher replied.

Crabapple came in and immediately began a harangue. "When are you going to get that door fixed?" he demanded. "Every time I come in here, that door sticks."

Looking over the meats in the display case, he

mumbled to himself, "Nothing looks fresh. Probably been sitting in there for weeks."

Finally, he said, "All right, no matter how bad your stuff looks, I'll take two small steaks. And this time, make them lean!"

"Yes, sir," the butcher replied. "In which direction?"

Comedian Red Buttons used to tell stories about his deprived childhood. "Every time I passed a butcher shop," he said, "I thought there had been a terrible accident."

• *Calories* •

"Doc, I'm here because I've decided I just have to do something about my weight."

"Well, that's a good first step. What have you tried?"

"First, I tried exercising. I do 20 sit-ups in the morning, and I walk home from the train at night."

"And . . . ?"

"It hasn't made a bit of difference. I'm still 40 pounds overweight."

"Exercise is fine. But if you don't cut down on your calorie intake, your weight won't go down."

"Well, if I have to, I have to."

"Okay, here's a diet I want you to follow. And I want you to follow it to the letter."

"I'll try."

"In three months, I want to see four-fifths of you for a checkup."

You know it's time to cut down on calories when
. . . you step on the scale and the readout says, "One at a time, please!

. . . you have to apply sunblock with a paint roller.

. . . you try to get out of bed and you rock yourself back to sleep in the process.

. . . Weight Watchers demands your resignation.

He: I can't understand what happens to all that money we put aside every month for groceries.
She: Go stand sideways in front of the mirror.

• *Children* •

The mother looked out the window, where her two boys were playing in the snow. She called the older boy to come inside.

"Alan," she said, "I've told you several times you have to share your toys with your little brother. You can't keep the sled to yourself."

"I am sharing it," Alan said. "I get to use the sled going down the hill, and he uses it going back up."

Like many three-year-olds, Juanita got no enjoyment out of being bathed. After a particularly vigorous scrubbing, her mother asked, "Don't you want to be a clean little girl?"

"Yes," Juanita said between sobs, "but can't you just dust me?"

Young Susie had developed the habit of saying "damn" every time something annoyed her. Her mother let it go the first few times she heard the word but eventually decided to put a stop to it.

"Susie," she said, "I don't want you using that word anymore. It's one of those words that people don't like to hear, especially from children. If you promise not to say it any more, I'll give you this quarter."

"Okay," Susie said. She took the quarter and went outside to play. Twenty minutes later, she was back.

"I was just playing with Diane," she said.

"That's nice," her mother said. "What did you two do together?"

"She taught me a word that's worth at least a dollar," Susie said.

Pushing a cart down a supermarket aisle, a man passed a woman whose cart carried a four-year-old girl. As he walked by, he heard the mother saying, "Take it easy, Natasha. It won't be long. We have only three more items to buy."

A few minutes later, he passed the same woman in another aisle. As the little girl looked at the items on the shelves, the woman crooned in a soothing voice, "It's okay, Natasha. We're almost finished. Nothing to get upset about, Tasha dear. We'll be outside in no time at all."

When the man reached the checkout counter, the woman was paying for her groceries. "Excuse me," he said. "I'd like to compliment you on the way you kept your daughter calm while you did your shopping. I overheard some of the soothing things you were saying to Natasha here to keep her from getting upset."

The woman looked puzzled for a few seconds, then laughed. "You've got it all wrong," she said. "My daughter's name is Kate. I'm Natasha."

A little boy was standing at the door of a house on tiptoe, trying very hard to reach the doorbell. A man passing by noticed this and stopped to help.

"Would you like me to ring the bell for you?" the man asked.

"Yes," the boy answered.

The man pressed the bell, smiled at the boy, and said, "Now what?"

"I don't know about you, mister," the boy said, "but I'm going to run like hell."

The teacher was trying to drum up enthusiasm among her third-grade students for the class picture. "Tell your parents you need to bring in five dollars by Friday. And keep in mind that many years from now, you'll love having this picture. You'll be able to look at it and say, 'There's Amanda. She's a famous doctor. And there's Robby, who made it into the movies.' "

One kid in the back of the room chimed in, "And there's the teacher. She's dead."

A woman sat in an airport, holding her six-month-old child. A man sat opposite them, stared at the baby for a long time, and said, "That's the ugliest baby I've ever seen."

"WHAT!" the woman screamed. "That's a vile thing to say! How dare you say a thing like that to me! You should be put in jail for such a vicious remark!"

A security guard came rushing up to her and said, "Easy, ma'am, take it easy, please. What seems to be the problem?"

Sobbing and gasping, the woman said, "Awful . . . just awful . . . never heard anything so terrible in my whole life. . . . that man. . . ."

"All right," the guard said, seeing that she was calming down. "Why don't you just sit right here. Sit down here and take it easy. Look, the man is gone. No need to think about him any more. Would you like me to get you a cup of water?"

Still sobbing, the woman said, "Yes, I would. Thank you very much."

"That's all right," the guard said. "I'll be right back with the water. And I'll tell you what—I'll even bring a banana for your monkey."

• *Diseases* •

Sherman came into the doctor's office and said heartily, "Well, Doc, what did the test results show?"

The doctor hesitated for a few seconds, then said, "Mr. Sherman, I have some good news and some bad news."

Sherman's face fell. "Tell me the bad news first," he said glumly.

The doctor took a deep breath and said, "I'm afraid you've come down with a very rare disease. No known cure. My estimate is that you have about six weeks to live."

Sherman stared into space and digested this information. Then he asked quietly, "And the good news?"

"My Internet stock just went through the roof," the doctor said, smiling.

After a series of tests, Patel went to see the foremost expert on heart disease in the U.S. "Doctor," he said, "I've been told I need a heart transplant. I've come to you because money is no object. I want the best treatment available, and I don't care what it costs."

The doctor looked at his list of transplants and

said, "I can let you have the heart of a 40-year-old who never drank or smoked and spent most of his adult life on a fat-free diet. This one would cost $25,000."

"Got anything better than that?" Patel asked.

"Yes," the doctor said. "Here's one from a 25-year-old man. Professional athlete, in great shape when he had a fatal accident. It'll cost you $100,000."

"I can go a lot higher," Patel said.

"Okay," the doctor said. "Here's one that would set you back $500,000. The man was 65 years old. Drank a quart of bourbon and smoked two packs of cigarettes every day. Never took care of his health in any way."

"Wait a minute," Patel said. "How could this one cost so much more than those others?"

"This one," the doctor said, "was never used. It was the heart of a lawyer."

→ *All right, so it's really a lawyer joke, not a disease joke. There are more good jokes about lawyers than about any other group on earth, and we want to make as many of them available to you as possible. So be on notice that we'll slip lawyer jokes into as many categories as we can.*

• *Detectives* •

Logan looked out the window of her jewelry store as a huge truck pulled up to the curb. The rear panel of the truck went up, and an elephant stepped out. Logan stared dumbfounded as the elephant rammed its head into her display window, brushed the broken glass aside, and used its trunk to suck up the jewels. Then the elephant turned and climbed into the truck. The rear panel came down, and the truck pulled away.

Fifteen minutes later, she recounted the incredible scene to Detective Ellis. When she was finished, he asked, "Can you describe the elephant?"

"Describe the elephant?" Logan said. "It was an elephant! What kind of description do you want?"

"There are two kinds of elephants," Ellis explained. "And one difference is in the ears. The Indian elephant has smaller ears than the African kind."

"Ears!" Logan said angrily. "How would I know about ears? The elephant had a stocking pulled over his head."

. . .

Detective Ramirez completed his tour of the burglarized store and said to the owner, "They certainly did a thorough job."

"They did," the owner said sadly. "They practically cleaned me out."

"We'll need a list of everything they took," Ramirez said.

"Sure," the owner said. Then he sighed and added, "I only wish they had done this yesterday."

"Why?"

"I wouldn't have lost as much," the owner said. "Yesterday everything was on sale."

• *Drivers* •

A traffic cop spots a car weaving from lane to lane on a busy highway. He takes off after the car and catches up with it in seconds. He's horrified to see that the driver is an old woman who's knitting as she drives.

"Pull over!" the cop shouts. "I said pull over!"

The woman turns to face him, smiles, and says, "No, actually, it's a scarf."

A haggard looking man stumbled into the Motor Vehicles office and asked where he should go to turn in his driver's license. "I can't drive in this city anymore," he explained. "I just don't have the vocabulary for it."

If you make a left turn from the right lane, you're probably careless—and not what the driver behind you said you are.

A car traveling several miles below the speed limit was causing horn-honking for miles. A traffic cop pulled the car over to the shoulder and spoke to the old man at the wheel.

"Do you realize you were driving 20 miles an hour?" the officer said. "The minimum speed on this highway is 40."

"But officer," the old man said, "that sign says 22."

"That sign says that this is Route 22," the officer explained. "It has nothing to do with the speed limit. By the way, your passengers back there don't look very good. Is anything wrong?"

"Oh," the old man said, "we just got off Route 120."

. . .

On Saturday night, Officer Wesley was staking out the local bar, fully anticipating having to write several tickets to drinkers who had failed to name a designated driver. Just after midnight, a man came staggering out of the bar. While Wesley watched, the man fell into the street, picked himself up, knocked over two garbage pails, then staggered to his car. He fumbled with his keys for several minutes before he managed to unlock his door and clamber inside. Then he proceeded to fall sound asleep at the wheel.

Wesley waited, ready to pounce as soon as the guy started his engine. The drivers of the other cars came out one at a time and drove off. When there were no other cars left, the guy woke up and started his car.

Wesley approached, explained that he was required to determine if the man was drunk, and proceeded to give him a Breathalyzer test. The test showed a blood-alcohol level of zero.

Wesley said, "Twenty minutes ago, you could hardly stand. And there's no alcohol in your blood? How come?"

The man explained, "Tonight was my turn to be the decoy."

• *Employment* •

A teenager went from door to door trying to earn money by doing odd jobs. After being turned away nine times, he hit pay dirt on the tenth try.

"Yes," the man said. "I need someone to paint my porch. You'll find two gallons of green paint in the garage, together with everything else you need."

"Fine," the boy said.

"I'll be working in the attic," the man said. "Ring the bell when the porch is finished."

About an hour later, the man came to the back door to answer the bell. "Finished so soon?" he said, surprised.

"Yep," the boy said. "But it looked more like a Ferrari than a Porsche."

The boss joined a group of her workers at the coffee urn and told a series of jokes she'd heard recently. Everybody laughed loudly. Everybody, that is, except Mike.

When she noticed that she was getting no reaction from him, the boss said, "What's the matter, Mike? No sense of humor?"

"My sense of humor is fine," he said. "But I don't have to laugh. I'm quitting tomorrow."

. . .

When Peters learned that he was being fired, he went to see the head of human resources. "Since I've been with the firm for so long," he said, "I think I deserve at least a letter of recommendation."

The human resources director agreed and said he'd have the letter the next day. The following morning, Peters found a letter on his desk. It read, "Jonathan Peters worked for our company for 11 years. When he left us, we were very satisfied."

Pam Worthy, CEO of Spiffy Software, was taking her daily half-hour power walk through the park outside her office building when she came across a young man sprawled on a park bench and sipping cola through a straw.

"How could a healthy young man like you just waste your time this way?" Pam said. "Why, you could be out selling soft drinks instead of sipping them."

"Why would I want to do that?" the young man asked.

"Think of it," she said. "Eventually, you could buy a small truck and deliver soft drinks all over the city."

"Why would I want to do that?"

"Well, you could build up the business until you had a whole fleet of trucks delivering all over the state."

"Why would I want to do that?"

"What's wrong with you?" Pam spouted. "If you worked hard enough, you could become the most successful soft drink distributor in the country—maybe even in the world!"

Once again, the young man asked calmly, "Why would I want to do that?"

"You fool!" Pam said. "With that kind of success, you could retire and spend the rest of your life relaxing and enjoying yourself."

The young man said, "But that's exactly what I'm doing now."

"Now, before I agree to take this job," the young applicant said, "I have one question. Are the hours long?"

"Well," the boss replied, "we try our best to keep them limited to 60 minutes."

• *Extraterrestrials* •

Two alien beings land their ship on the roof of an office building and make their way down to the sidewalk. It's late at night and no one is around, so they decide to scout the area. They walk into a bank lobby lit up with the glow of a waiting ATM screen.

One of the aliens walks up to the screen and, in his smoothest voice, says to the ATM, "What's a beautiful creature like you doing in a place like this?"

Outside the bank lobby, the same two aliens stop to look at a parking meter. One of them picks up a quarter from the ground and, after a little trial and error, inserts the quarter into the meter.

When he sees the dial move, he says to his companion, "How about that? I weigh an hour."

✦ *Food* ✦

At his local fruit stand, Henry put five apples in a bag and stepped up to the counter. "These apples are awfully small," he said, putting money on the counter.

"I guess they are," the owner said, giving him his change.

Henry took a bite out of one and made a face. "They don't taste very good, either," he said.

The owner nodded. "Good thing they're so small, isn't it?" he said.

Younger Scout: How can I tell the difference between a mushroom and a toadstool?

Older Scout: Just eat one before you go to bed. If you wake up the next morning, it was a mushroom.

Max and Matilda were at a charity buffet dinner. When Max sat down with his overloaded plate, Matilda said, "That's the fourth time you've filled your plate. Aren't you embarrassed?"

"Nope," Max said, his mouth full of food. "I just keep telling them it's for my wife."

. . .

A seedy beggar approached a well-dressed woman in front of her office building. "Excuse me, ma'am," he said. "Can you let me have $1,500 for a meal?"

"$1,500!" she gasped. "Why, you can get a decent meal for less than $10."

"I was hoping to have it at one of those Parisian restaurants I've read so much about," he said.

A man goes into an ice cream parlor and says, "I'd like two scoops of chocolate ice cream, please."

The girl behind the counter says, "I'm very sorry, sir, but our delivery truck broke down this morning. We're out of chocolate."

"In that case," the man says, "I'll have two scoops of chocolate ice cream."

"You don't understand, sir," the girl says. "We have no chocolate."

"Then just give me some chocolate," he says.

Getting angrier by the second, the girl says, "Sir, will you spell VAN, as in vanilla?"

The man says, "V-A-N."

"Now spell STRAW, as in strawberry."

"OK. S-T-R-A-W."

"Now," the girl says, "spell STINK, as in chocolate."

The man hesitates. Then he says, "There is no stink in chocolate."

"THAT'S WHAT I'VE BEEN TRYING TO TELL YOU!" she screams.

• *Funerals* •

Two golf enthusiasts were walking down the fairway when a funeral procession passed by on the road. One of the players stopped, took off his cap, and watched solemnly as the cars slowly passed by. When the last car was out of sight, he put his cap back on.

His friend said, "That was very touching, to see you pay your respects like that to a passing funeral."

"Yeah, well," the first player said, "we would have been married 20 years next month."

"We are gathered here today," the priest said, "to pay final homage to a good man. He was a kind man, a man whom everyone loved, a man who treasured his family as his family treasured him."

The widow of the deceased leaned over and

whispered to her grandson, "Go up and make sure it's Grandpa in that coffin."

When his father died, Martin told the funeral director to spare no expense. So when, a month after the funeral, a bill arrived for $12,000, Martin paid it without hesitation. The next month, he received a bill for $85, and he paid it, figuring something had been left off the original bill. But a month after that, a new bill for $85 arrived. This time, Martin called the funeral director.

"You said you wanted the best funeral we could arrange," the director told him. "So I rented him a tuxedo."

When Sadie's husband of 45 years died in his sleep, she handled things with her usual efficiency. She had the undertaker remove the body, she washed the sheets and made up the bed, and she left the house to go to the newspaper office to file an obituary notice.

As she stepped out the door, Sadie stood in front of the only piece of property her husband left as a memorial of their 45 years together. She took a long look at his battered 1983 pickup truck. Then she walked into town.

The clerk at the newspaper office gave her a form to fill out. True to her habit of efficiency, Sadie wrote, "Billy Bob Mannion died today."

"You have to pay for a minimum of ten words," the clerk said. "Is there some additional sentiment you'd like to include?"

After a moment's thought, Sadie added to her announcement so that it read, "Billy Bob Mannion died today. 1983 pickup truck for sale."

Everyone agreed that Clarence Mudge was the meanest man in town. He kicked dogs and cats, threw stones at children who played near his property, and even waved his cane threateningly at babies in strollers. When Mudge died, no one mourned him, but a lot of people showed up at the funeral service, possibly to celebrate.

"Mr. Mudge is gone," the priest said, "and I would like someone to come up front and give a short eulogy in his honor."

The priest waited, but no one stirred.

"Oh, come now," the priest said, "there must be someone here who can say a good word about this man."

Dead silence.

Moving from annoyance toward anger, the priest said, "I can't believe that no one in this entire congregation can think of a single positive thing to say at the funeral of this man."

Finally, someone in the last row stood up. He was an old man, possibly even older than Clarence Mudge. He cleared his throat and said, "He wasn't as bad as his brother."

• *Ghosts* •

When Reuben Forrest died, the owner of the Shangri-La closed the restaurant for a day, the only time he'd done that in 50 years. Reuben was the first employee hired by the restaurant, and he was a minor legend among the city's waiters.

He was so much of a legend, in fact, that the waiters' union agreed to sponsor a seance to see if Reuben's ghost could be contacted. Four of his oldest friends—all waiters—went to a medium, who sat them around a table and ordered everyone to hold hands.

"The only way to contact Reuben," the medium explained, is for all of us to close our eyes and intone his full name in unison."

With eyes closed, the four friends and the

medium said in one voice, "Reuben Forrest." Nothing happened.

They repeated his name. Still nothing. They called him a third time, then a fourth. When they chanted his name a fifth time, a dim light appeared over the table, and a voice said, "Yes. I'm here."

"It's him!" one of the waiters exclaimed. "That's Reuben's voice! But Reuben, why did we have to call you five times before you responded?"

"Because," the voice said angrily, "this is not my table!"

→ *Yes, you'll find the same punch line—with a different joke—in the section titled* **Restaurants** *beginning on p. 75. Just goes to show how flexible a good joke can be.*

Glamis had written several books on his success at contacting the dead, but he was constantly attacked by skeptics. Determined to show them up, he set out to capture a photographic image of a ghost.

He went at midnight to a house known to be haunted, waited until he heard some noises, then followed the sounds to the stairway. There at the top of the stairs was—no mistake about it—a genuine ghost.

As Glamis fumbled with his camera, he could see the ghost waving, smiling, even posing for pictures. This had to be the most cooperative ghost ever to show his visage to the world.

The light was very weak, so Glamis simply pressed the button for shot after shot after shot. Then the ghost vanished.

When he developed the film, Glamis was crushed to see that the dim light had killed any chance of getting a usable photo. He wrote in his notebook, "The spirit was willing, but the flash was weak."

Wolfgang and Fred, both past 80, had been best friends for over half a century. As Fred lay dying, Wolfgang whispered into his ear.

"Fred, I want a favor. If you get to heaven, I want you to try to contact me to tell me one thing."

"Anything," Fred said weakly. "What do you want to know?"

"I want to know if they have baseball in heaven."

Fred smiled, nodded, and quietly passed away.

The next night, Wolfgang was awakened by a disembodied voice calling his name.

"Who's there?" Wolfgang asked.

"It's me, Wolfie. It's Fred. And I have some good news and some bad news."

"Fred! This is terrific! The good news first."

"I'm happy to report that there is baseball in heaven."

"Wonderful!" Wolfgang exclaimed. "And the bad news?"

"Day after tomorrow, you're our starting pitcher."

• *God* •

An amateur hiker loses his footing, slips off the edge of a cliff, and is saved from death only by grabbing onto a large branch. He doesn't have the strength to pull himself up, and he can't bring himself to look down.

So he prays. "Lord, please help me. I'm losing my strength, and I can't hold on much longer."

A booming voice from above says, "I am the Lord."

"Save me, Lord," the hiker cries out.

"I will," the voice says. "First, prove your faith in me by letting go of the branch."

The hiker looks down at the endless expanse below him. Then he looks up and says, "Is there anyone else up there?"

In the Garden of Eden, Adam makes it known to the Lord that he's lonely. "I have decided to give you a companion," the Lord says. "She will be beautiful, intelligent, and witty. And she will obey your every command, do anything to make you happy."

"Great!" says Adam. "What do I have to do in return?"

"It will cost you an arm and a leg," the Lord says.

"That's pretty steep," Adam says. "What can I get for a rib?"

Why did God create man before he created woman? He needed a rough draft so he could perfect the final version.

• *Holidays* •

Coming home from work one night in early December, Susan saw an envelope taped to her apartment door. She took it down and found a Christmas card inside. It read, "Happy holidays from your super."

"What a friendly gesture," she thought.

The following week, she found another envelope on her door, with the same card inside. This time the message said, "Happy holidays from your super. Second notice."

After polishing off a solid chocolate Easter bunny, five-year-old Timmy said, "I like Easter better than Halloween."

"Why?" his mother asked. "You get just as much candy on both days."

"Yeah, but on Easter, you don't have to ring a lot of doorbells to get it."

Why is Christmas like a day at the office? You do all the work and the fat guy in the suit gets all the credit.

• *Hotels* •

McAllister arrived in Las Vegas without a hotel reservation, and he'd spent the last two hours flitting from one hotel to another looking for a room. By the time he reached the fifth hotel, he was determined to do anything to get a place to sleep.

"I'm sorry, sir," the desk clerk said. "We simply don't have a room available."

"A cot," McAllister said. "I'll take a cot in the space you reserve for employees who have to work overnight."

"We had one two hours ago," the clerk replied. "It's gone now."

"The Presidential suite. I'll pay whatever it takes."

"Sorry, sir. Even that's gone."

"Now, look," McAllister said. "Suppose the Sultan of Brunei suddenly showed up. Do you mean to tell me you wouldn't have a room for him?"

"Well," the clerk said thoughtfully. "I have to admit, for the Sultan of Brunei, we probably would be able to find something."

"Good!" McAllister said. "The Sultan can't make it. Give me his room!"

• *Ignorance* •

A ventriloquist was working at a church social, when a man in the audience stood up to complain. "I'm sick of this!" the man said. "You've been making nasty remarks about how everybody in this town is stupid, and I don't want to hear any more!"

Stunned, the ventriloquist said, "I'm really sorry, sir. This was all being done in fun. I had no intention of hurting anyone's feelings."

"You shut up!" the man spouted. "I was talking to that little wise guy sitting on your knee!"

Larry and Harry—sometimes known to their friends as Dim and Dimmer—drove 500 miles to go fishing. They paid a huge sum to rent a cabin, then a similar amount to rent a boat. They fished for three days and caught only one fish between them.

On the way home, Harry fiddled with a calculator while Larry drove. After an hour, Harry said, "Do you realize that this one fish we caught cost us almost $2,000?"

"Wow!" Larry said. "It's a good thing we didn't catch any more."

. . .

The next time they went fishing, Dim and Dimmer had better luck, catching a boatload of fish. "This is great," Dim said. "Why don't we come back to this same spot tomorrow?"

"Very good idea," Dimmer said, a little surprised that his buddy could come up with something that good. So Dimmer took out a piece of chalk to put a large X on the side of the boat.

Dim shook his head. "That's probably the dumbest thing I've seen all month," he said.

"Why?" Dimmer asked.

"How can you be sure that we'll get the same boat tomorrow?"

How do you make a dolt happy in his old age?
   Tell him some good jokes when he's young.

Dim and Dimmer once tried their hand at selling Christmas trees. They bought enough to fill their pickup truck, then sold the trees for less than they had paid.

After three truckloads, Dim said, "You know, we're not going to make any money this way. We sell these trees for less than it costs us."

Dimmer wrinkled his brow and thought as hard as he could. Finally, he said, "I guess we better get a bigger truck."

"Spell 'Mississippi.'"

"Uh—the river, or the state?"

Dim and Dimmer are at a shopping mall, having just parked the car.

"Darn!" says Dim. "I locked the keys in the car!"

"Then we'll have to break one of the windows to get at them," Dimmer says.

"Don't even say that!" Dim says.

"Well," says Dimmer, "maybe we can get a wire hanger and use that to unlock the door."

"That never works," Dim says.

"Well, you better think of something!" Dimmer says. "It's starting to rain, and the top is down."

A couple of days later, Dim and Dimmer were supposed to meet at one of the department stores in that same mall. Dim never showed up, so Dimmer went home. When they got together that night, Dimmer asked what had happened.

"It was terrible," Dim said. "I was on the escalator, coming to meet you, and suddenly, the escalator stopped running. I stood there for over an hour while they fixed it."

"You stood on the escalator for an hour while they fixed it?" Dimmer asked incredulously.

"Yes," Dim said. "What else could I do?"

"Dummy!" Dimmer said. "Why didn't you sit down?"

"How's your search for a new house going?"

"Well, I try to remember what the real estate brokers all say."

"What's that?"

"In real estate, there are only three factors to keep in mind. Location, location, and—darn, I always have trouble remembering that third one."

The contractor had agreed to let his nephew work with him for the summer, even though the kid showed no intellectual promise whatsoever. The contractor parked his truck outside the lumber yard and sent the kid inside to make the purchase.

Reading from his uncle's list, the kid said, "I want 200 two-by-fours eight feet long, 120 one-by-eights, six feet long, and 240 two-by-sixes."

The clerk waited a few seconds, then asked, "How long? How long do you want them?"

The kid pondered for nearly half a minute. Then he said confidently, "Forever. We're building a house."

Auerbach knew it was a mistake when he agreed to do it, but a friend is a friend. "My nephew's looking for a job," his neighbor said. Auerbach said the young man could work in his factory.

But the nephew didn't seem to know enough to get across the street unassisted. Auerbach had put him on six different tasks in the factory, and he'd made a mess of each of them. Now Auerbach was staring down at a broken machine that would cost a small fortune to have repaired.

"Astounding!" Auerbach said. "It just amazes me how you can turn everything you touch to garbage. Tell me, what's your IQ?"

"I think . . . it's . . . 20-20," the nephew said.

• *Investments* •

Sturbridge was tired of reading about all those people making a killing in the stock market while his broker, a very conservative man, always talked him out of plunging into speculation.

"Enough of this blue chip stuff," Sturbridge told the broker over the phone. "I want to get into some of these Internet stocks that will triple my money in a week."

"If you insist, I can't refuse," the broker said. "But this is August."

"So what?" Sturbridge asked.

"Well, August is one of the most dangerous months for getting into speculative stocks."

"It is?" Sturbridge said. "What are the other ones?"

"From January to July and September to December," the broker said.

While the brokers were busily calling potential customers to drum up business, the president of the firm stopped to eavesdrop on a new employee. He listened as the young man talked eight consecutive contacts into moving their stock portfolios to him.

The boss approached the young man and said, "I've been listening in, and I must say I'm impressed with your ability. Where did you learn so much about talking to investors?"

"Yale, sir," the young man answered.

Impressed, the boss said, "Oh, that's fine, just fine. And what's your name?"

"Yackson," he replied.

• *Journalism* •

Back in 1889, a young reporter learned a lesson about the dangers of overwriting in reporting the news. He was witness to the flood in Johnstown, Pennsylvania, and he began his article, "God sat on a hill here last night and watched disaster and death sweep through this community."

His editor wired back, "Forget the flood. Interview God."

Many viewers of TV news have to make the daily decision of whether to watch the 6 o'clock news and suffer from indigestion, or the 11 o'clock news and put up with insomnia.

• *Justice* •

The murder trial had not gone well for the notorious gangster. There was so much evidence against him that he couldn't believe the jury would acquit him. So he instructed his underlings to bribe one of the jurors to hold out for a conviction of manslaughter.

It took the jurors 18 days of deliberation, but they finally returned with a conviction of one count of manslaughter. Outside, one of the gangster's henchmen took the juror aside.

"You did good," he said. "But why did it take 18 days?"

"It was a tough battle," the juror said. "Everybody else wanted to acquit him."

"Is there any reason you should not serve on this jury?" the lawyer asked.

"Yes, there is," Linda replied. "I don't believe in capital punishment."

The judge cleared his throat and said, "That isn't relevant in this situation, ma'am. This is a civil case in which a wife is suing her husband for losing their life savings at the racetrack."

Linda thought for a few seconds, then said,

"There's no reason I shouldn't serve. I could be wrong about capital punishment."

• *Language* •

The community was radically divided over the question of whether to include sex education in the elementary school curriculum. At a public hearing, parents heard the whole spectrum of opinions, from open and frank discussion of every aspect of sex to an absolute ban on anything even approaching the subject.

Finally, one cranky old woman, known throughout the town for her contrarian views, surprised everyone by announcing that she was in favor of sex education in elementary school.

"Teach them what they have to know," she said. "But remember that eight years old is too young to be calling things by their right names."

A mother made the mistake of saying to her very literate teenage daughter, "All you do is complain."

"Not true," the daughter responded. "I also

grumble, make a fuss, carp, protest, beef, squawk, and sometimes even demur."

If you speak three languages, you're trilingual.
  If you speak two languages, you're bilingual.
  If you speak one language, you're American.

Cindy was new in town, still trying to find her way around. She walked up to a man standing outside the school building. "Can you tell me where the library's at?" she asked.

The man stared down at her, raised his eyebrows, and said in his stuffiest voice, "Young lady, it is not proper to end a sentence with a preposition."

Cindy stared back at him. Then she said, "Can you tell me where the library's at, jerk?"

Back in the days when the Soviet Union was terrorized by the KGB, an agent burst into the room of a citizen who was under investigation. The agent was delighted to have caught the man reading a Bible.

"This book is written in Hebrew. Why are you reading it?" the agent demanded.

"When I die and go to heaven," the man replied, "I want to know how to speak the language.

The agent sneered and said, "And what if you go to hell?"

"I already speak Russian," the man said.

George Bernard Shaw said that England and the United States are two countries separated by the same language.

• *Lawyers* •

The pope and a lawyer arrive at the gates of heaven at the same time. St. Peter says, "Your Holiness, I'll show you to your room first."

With the lawyer tagging along, St. Peter leads the pope to a comfortable little room with a bed, a night table, two chairs, and a bookcase. The pope thanks him and goes into the room.

St. Peter then leads the lawyer to a sumptuous suite with chandeliers, a wide-screen TV, a sauna, piped-in music, and a staff of servants.

"Incredible!" the lawyer says. "But I don't understand. Why did the pope get such a bare-bones room, while I get all this luxury?"

St. Peter replied, "We get plenty of popes up here, but you're the first lawyer we've seen in a couple of centuries."

Another lawyer shows up in heaven, and St. Peter offers him a wheelchair. "Why would I need a wheelchair?" the lawyer asks.

"We've been monitoring your work," St. Peter says. "Based on the number of hours you've billed clients for, you should be 147 years old."

"Are you a lawyer?"

"Yes, I am."

"How much do you charge?"

"A thousand dollars for four questions."

"Isn't that pretty steep?"

"Yes, it is. What's your fourth question?"

Each kid in kindergarten stands up to tell the class what mommy and daddy do for a living. When Stephen announces, "My father is a professional killer," the teacher gags but says nothing.

That evening, the teacher calls Stephen's home

and tells his father what the boy said in class. The father is amused.

"Don't be alarmed," he tells the teacher. "I'm actually an attorney. But I can't tell that to a five-year-old child."

As the lawyer came out of the anesthesia, he opened his eyes and said, "Doctor, why are the blinds drawn so tightly?"

"There's a major fire across the street," the doctor explained. "We didn't want you to wake up and think the operation was a failure."

A metalwork factory receives an order for two dozen cages, 6 feet long, 12 feet wide, and 7 feet high. The worker delivers the cages to a chemical laboratory and asks what they're going to be used for.

The scientist says, "We're testing some chemicals on a group of lawyers."

Puzzled, the worker asks, "But don't you usually use rats for that kind of thing?"

"Yes," the scientist says. "But these are very dangerous chemicals, and you get so attached to rats."

. . .

Have you heard about the lawyer with a con-
science?
   Neither has anyone else.

What do you call a dozen lawyers at the bottom of
the ocean?
   A good beginning.

Why are there so many lawyers in Washington,
D.C., and so many toxic waste dumps in New Jer-
sey?
   New Jersey got first choice.

Satan: Promise me your soul and the souls of
everyone in your immediate family, and I'll make
you a senior partner in the firm.
   Lawyer: So . . . what's the catch?

How many lawyers does it take to shingle a roof?
   Depends on how thinly you slice them.

• *Machines* •

Software developers work day and night to make computers appear as much as possible like intelligent humans. But sometimes they get carried away with their task.

One interactive program designed to teach math concepts to first graders includes a series of responses that a computer gives after getting an incorrect response from a kid. One of these responses is: INCORRECT. TRY AGAIN. AND REMEMBER, THE FACT THAT I SAID YOU WERE WRONG DOESN'T MEAN I DON'T LOVE YOU.

Larry and Harry (you might remember them as Dim and Dimmer) were on a cross-country flight when the pilot announced, "Sorry, folks, but we've lost one of our four engines. This means we're likely to be about 30 minutes late."

Ten minutes later, the pilot, sounding a bit more concerned, announced, "It seems a second engine has gone out. I'm afraid you'll have to plan on being over an hour late."

A few minutes after that, the pilot came on again, this time sounding very strained. "Ladies and gentlemen, a third engine has just failed."

"Darn!" said Larry. "If we lose that fourth one, we'll be over two hours late!"

• *Marriage* •

"Cheryl, if I died, would you marry again?"
  "Yes."
  "And would you let him into my house?"
  "Sure."
  "Would he sleep in my bed?"
  "I guess he would."
  "Would he use my golf clubs?"
  "Nope."
  "Really? Why not?"
  "Because he's left-handed."

Wendy and Tim had been dating off and on for years, and now here he was, on bended knee, proposing marriage. "I knew this would happen sooner or later," Wendy thought. "What do I do now?"

  "Wendy," Tim repeated. "I want you to be my wife."

"I'm sorry, Tim," Wendy said. "I just can't marry you."

"Why not? Is there someone else?"

"Oh . . . there must be, Tim. There just must be!"

Doris accompanied her husband to the doctor for his annual checkup. While he was getting dressed, the doctor came out to the reception area to speak privately with Doris.

"I don't like the way your husband looks," he said softly.

"Neither do I," she replied, "but he's handy to have around the house."

Puffing away on an exercise bike at the health club, Edna said to her friend, "My husband insists I come here twice a week. He'd rather be with a woman with a slim figure."

"What's wrong with that?" her friend asked.

"He likes to be with her when I'm here!" Edna said.

Marriage is nature's way of keeping people from fighting with strangers.

. . .

Sarah was reading a newspaper, while her husband was engrossed in a magazine. Suddenly, she burst out laughing.

"Listen to this," she said. "There's a classified ad here where a guy is offering to swap his wife for a season ticket to the stadium."

"Hmmm," her husband said, not looking up from his magazine.

Teasing him, Sarah said, "Would you swap me for a season ticket?"

"Absolutely not," he said.

"How sweet," Sarah said. "Tell me why not."

"Season's more than half over," he said.

Two co-workers were sharing some intimacies over drinks. One of them blurted out, "I didn't sleep with my wife before we were married. How about you?"

The other replied, "I don't know. What was her maiden name?"

A husband and wife were driving to a mall 50 miles from home. Their six-year-old daughter sat in the backseat listening to the exchanges that took place between them.

At the mall, the husband stopped into a shoe store. The girl looked up at her mother and said, "Mom, before you met Dad, who told you how to drive?"

He takes his wife wherever he goes, so he never has to kiss her good-bye.

"William, I just won the lottery! Pack your bags!"

"That's great, honey! Should I pack for the beach, the mountains, or what?"

"Who cares? Just get out."

• *Medical Care* •

The reception area of the doctor's office was filled to capacity, but the doctor was working at his usual snail's pace. After waiting two hours, an old man slowly stood up and headed for the door. When everyone stopped talking to look at him, he

announced, "I guess I'll just go home and die a
natural death."

"Good morning, Doctor."

"Mr. Farrier, what happened to you? You look
terrible!"

"You told me to take that medicine for three
days, then to skip a day."

"Yes?"

"That skipping nearly killed me."

Three nurses at the gate of heaven are asked
what they did during their lives. The first nurse
says, "Aside from my regular work as a nurse,
I did charity work most weekends, helping
old people who couldn't get around on their
own."

"Wonderful," St. Peter says. "Come on in and
enjoy eternity."

The second nurse says, "I worked in an emergency room for 20 years, and I tried to give com-
fort to people in terrible situations."

"Very good," says St. Peter. "Come right in."

The third nurse says, "For the last five years, I
worked as a managed care nurse for an HMO."

St. Peter studies his clipboard for a few seconds, then says, "I can approve you only for a five-day stay."

"You're going to need surgery immediately," the doctor said.

"How much is this going to cost me?"

"About $10,000."

"But doctor, I haven't got that kind of money!"

"Don't worry. You don't have to pay it all at once. We'll agree to a figure, and you can pay me that amount every month."

"Oh . . . like you're buying a car?"

"Well, actually, a boat."

Doctor: I have bad news. You have a fatal disease.

Patient: How long do I have to live, doctor?

Doctor: Ten.

Patient: Ten what?

Doctor: Nine, eight, seven. . . .

A general practitioner, a psychiatrist, a surgeon, and a pathologist went duck hunting. It wasn't long before they saw a bird fly over.

The GP raised his rifle, aimed, and said, "I'm not really sure that's a duck." He didn't fire.

The psychiatrist raised his rifle, aimed, and said, "I know it's a duck, but does the duck know it's a duck?" He didn't fire.

The surgeon raised his rifle, aimed, and fired. The bird fell to the ground. The surgeon turned to the pathologist and said, "Go see if that's a duck."

"Tell me what your symptoms are, Mr. Nelson."

"Well, doctor, I have this constant ringing in my ears and, as you can see, my eyes bulge out."

"Hmmm. Get undressed and let me examine you."

After a thorough examination, the doctor said, "This is a serious condition you have, Mr. Nelson. The only treatment I know of is a very delicate surgical operation. It's going to cost you in excess of $200,000."

"Two hun—but doctor, I don't have that kind of money!"

"Why don't you take a day or two to think about it?" the doctor says.

Nelson talks it over with his wife, and they agree to have the operation done. They mortgage their home, borrow the money, and pay the doctor in advance.

After the surgery, Nelson feels like a new man.

The symptoms are gone. He's so thrilled he decides to do something he's never done before. He telephones an expensive tailor and says, "Come to my hospital room with your tape measure. I want an entire new wardrobe of custom-made clothes.

The tailor shows up and looks Nelson up and down. "I don't need a tape measure," he says. "You wear a size 42 jacket, with a half-inch taken out in the lower back. Your sleeves are 35 inches long. For the pants, 39 ¼ waist, and 33 inches long."

"That's astounding!" Nelson says.

"And the underwear, 40-inch waist."

"That's your only mistake," Nelson says. I wear size 38 underwear."

"No mistake," the tailor says. "I've been in this business 50 years. Underwear size 40."

"Afraid not," Nelson says. "I've been wearing size 38 for years."

"Impossible," the tailor says. "You wear size 38, you'll have a constant ringing in your ears and your eyes will bulge out."

• *Narcissism* •

A famous actress came into her lawyer's office two weeks after her wedding. "I want you to begin divorce proceedings," she said.

"Divorce?" the lawyer said. "But you just got married. How could things have gone wrong so quickly?"

"They went wrong almost immediately," the actress said. "At the church, he signed his name in the register in bigger letters than mine."

Louise hated blind dates and here she was, stuck in one that seemed it would never end. They'd been together three hours, and this guy had talked about nothing but I and Me, Me and I.

Finally, through the haze of her boredom, Louise heard what might be a sign of relief. "But enough about me," he said. "Let's talk about you."

Louise perked up until he added, "What do you think about me?"

• *Offices* •

The CEO was over 90, and the other executives in the company had spent years pretending they didn't notice that he'd passed into senility. One day at a board meeting, he addressed one of his longtime vice presidents.

"Smithers," he growled, "you look different. You're not wearing your glasses. And your hair doesn't look the way it usually does. And that tie—you don't wear ties like that, Smithers."

"Excuse me, sir," the VP said. "I—I'm . . . not . . . Smithers."

"Good heavens!" the old man exclaimed. "You've even changed your name!"

"Everything in your application seems to be in order, Mr. Wiggins," the interviewer said. "Now, before we go any further, let me explain one of our hiring policies. We look for interesting people with special skills. Is there anything special we should know that wouldn't show up on this application?"

"Well, yes, there is," Wiggins said. "I've recently won two trivia contests, and I've completed the daily crossword puzzle in less than ten minutes."

"That is interesting," said the interviewer, "but I was thinking more along the lines of things you'd do in the office."

"Oh, those were during office hours."

• *Optimists* •

An optimist is someone who believes the housefly is desperately looking for a way out.

A dolt fell from the 30th floor of an office building, and as he passed the 10th floor, a friend yelled, "Hey, Irv, how's it going?"

"Pretty good so far!" he called back.

• *Pain* •

The patient lifts his hand above his head and says, "Doctor, it hurts every time I go like this."

"Well, don't go like that," the doctor says.

. . .

"Doctor, I have a terrible pain in my right foot."
   "Have you ever had this pain before?"
   "Yes."
   "Well, you've got it again."

• *Plumbers* •

Hogan had just finished cleaning out Mrs. Sanchez's septic tank. He was still wiping off his hands when Mrs. Sanchez said, "You always do very good work for us, Mr. Hogan. Tell me, is plumbing the field you always wanted to go into?"

   "As a matter of fact," Hogan said, when I was an apprentice, I wanted to go to medical school. I dreamed of becoming a neurosurgeon."

   "What made you give up the dream?" Mrs. Sanchez asked.

   Handing her the bill, he answered, "I couldn't afford the cut in pay."

In my experience, an absent-minded plumber is one who answers an emergency call with his tools in hand.

• *Quarrels* •

He did something really stupid. She chewed him out for it. He apologized. They made up.

However, from time to time, she mentioned what he had done. "Honey," he said, "why do you keep bringing that up? I thought your policy was 'forgive and forget.'"

"It is," she said. "I just don't want you to forget that I've forgiven and forgotten."

They quarreled about money and went to bed angry. The next morning, they rose, showered, dressed, and ate breakfast in silence. Finally, hoping to break the ice, he said, "You know, honey, I'm not myself today."

"Really?" she said. "I hadn't noticed the improvement."

• *Restaurants* •

A man walks into a restaurant and says, "How do you prepare your chickens?"

The owner looks at him and says, "We don't do anything special. We just tell them they're going to die."

"Waiter! Waiter! That woman seems to be having a heart attack!"

"Sorry, sir, that's not my table."

➜ *The next one isn't really a restaurant joke, but it follows nicely upon the preceding joke.*

"Aesop," the young Greek child said, "please tell us a story."

"Certainly," Aesop replied. "Which one would you like to hear?"

"Tell us the one about the three bears."

"Sorry," Aesop said. "That's not my fable."

Playwright George S. Kaufman was notoriously demanding of quick service from waiters. Among his attempts to put them in their place was his proposed tombstone epitaph for a slow waiter: *God finally caught his eye.*

• *Riddles* •

Why don't cannibals eat comedians?
   They taste funny.

Why is doing nothing so tiring?
   Because you can't stop and rest.

What are two things you can't have for breakfast?
   Lunch and dinner.

How many legs does a horse have if you call its
tail a leg?
   Four. Calling a tail a leg doesn't make it one.

How do you get down from an elephant?
   You don't. You get it from a duck.

How can you keep an angry rhino from charging?
   Take away its credit cards.

• *Science* •

The college president asked the chairman of the physics department to come to his office. "This budget request," the president said, "is staggering. Every year, your department needs new—and very expensive—equipment."

"Well," the chairman said, "it is physics, after all. We have to keep up."

"I know, I know," said the president, "but I wish you could be more like the math department. Once they got their computers, they haven't asked for much more than pencils, paper, and erasers."

Smiling, the physics chairman said, "We could even try to emulate the philosophy department. I understand they don't even bother requesting erasers."

That same physics chairman sat opposite a teenage boy on a train ride, and after they'd struck up a conversation, the boy asked the professor what he did for a living.

"I study science," the professor said.

"Study science!" the boy said. "Why, I finished that in tenth grade."

Research scientists may be the only people in the world who are considered to be doing something useful when they don't know what they're doing.

• *Shipwrecks* •

He called himself Mysto, and he was a pretty good magician, who performed mostly on cruise ships. This particular trip was complicated by the fact that he was saddled with a parrot who specialized in wisecracks. He was minding the bird for his brother, and he'd promised not to let it out of his sight. As a result, the bird was onstage during Mysto's act.

When Mysto made an egg disappear, the bird squawked, "He's got it in his pocket."

Mysto produced a rabbit out of thin air, and the bird announced, "Awwk! It was under the table all the time."

As Mysto prepared for his big finale, he thought of ways of doing the bird in. But he remembered his promise to his brother, and he went on with the act.

"Now, ladies and gentlemen, prepare for an astonishing event, unlike anything you've ever seen before." At the moment that Mysto waved his scarf in the air, the ship ran into a reef. Within seconds, the alarms went off, followed by instructions to enter the lifeboats.

Twenty minutes later, Mysto paddled toward a lifeboat, one arm wrapped around a fragment of a beam. A smaller piece of wood floated between him and the boat, with the parrot perched on it.

As the two neared each other, the parrot said, "All right, you've got me. What did you do with the ship?"

One of the lifeboats carrying survivors of that wreck was within sight of land, but surrounded by several sharks. "We'll never get to shore," one of the passengers cried.

A lawyer stood up and said, "Maybe you won't, but I will."

He dove into the water and began swimming to shore. As he did, the sharks parted from each other, creating a lane for the lawyer to swim through.

"I don't believe it!" one of the passengers gasped. "Why don't those sharks attack that lawyer?"

"Professional courtesy," someone else explained.

• *Taxis* •

Ronnie and Lonnie scored big at a Las Vegas casino—nearly a quarter of a million dollars. "I can't wait to get back to New York and let everybody know," Lonnie said. "Let's call the airport right now."

"No," Ronnie said. "Let's go like a couple of rich guys. "We'll buy a Rolls and drive to New York."

"I have a better idea!" Lonnie said. "We'll go like a couple of rich guys with money to burn. We'll take a cab!"

They hailed a taxi, told the driver what they had in mind, and agreed to pay double the meter fare, so he could get back to Vegas. Then Lonnie held the door open for Ronnie to get in.

"Wait," Ronnie said. "I'm going up to 62^d Street. You get out at 43^d, so you better get in first."

A man who'd had a few drinks got into a cab and gave the driver an address on the other side of town. When they reached the destination, the cab driver had to yell to wake him up.

"We're here," the driver said. "That'll be $7.50."

The passenger spent several minutes emptying out his pockets and finally announced, "Sorry, bud. I have only $6."

Annoyed, the driver said, "Well, the fare is $7.50."

"Tell you what," the passenger said. "Take the 6 bucks, back up about four blocks, leave me there, and we'll call it even."

A taxi driver and a minister arrived in heaven at the same time. The taxi driver was led to a palatial suite, and the minister was given a postage-stamp–sized room.

"I don't understand," the minister said. "All he did was drive a cab. I was in the ministry for four decades."

"Up here," St. Peter said, "we go by results. "While you preached, people slept. While he drove, people prayed."

• *Ukuleles* •

➜ *Among musicians, players of certain instruments are the objects of many, many jokes.*

Those who play classical music, for example, exchange vast numbers of jokes about violists. Jazz musicians tend to pick on trombonists and drummers. In the country-western field, banjo players are the victims of choice. Most of these jokes, of course, have nothing to do with the instruments or the people who actually play them. With that in mind, we've adapted some of them to apply to ukulele players.

What did the ukulele player say to the dentist?
  This might hurt a little.

What's the definition of perfect pitch?
  Throwing a ukulele into the dumpster without having it touch the sides.

Son: When I grow up, I want to play the ukulele.
  Father: Sorry, but you can't have it both ways.

What's the difference between a ukulele and a car?
  You can tune a car.

. . .

A policeman walking his beat saw a man violently shaking a young boy by the shoulders. "Cut that out!" the policeman ordered. "What's going on here?"

The man let the boy go. "Officer," he said, "I was playing my ukulele, and when I put it down, this kid sneaked up and twisted one of the tuning pegs."

"I see why you're annoyed," the cop said, "but is that any reason to get violent with the kid?"

"Maybe not," the man said. "But the little stinker won't tell me which peg!"

• *Vacations* •

Barbara and Will decided that this was the year to do something different for vacation. After considering several possibilities, they decided on a cruise.

Their first reaction was awe. The size of the ship, the luxurious accommodations, and the friendly staff all combined to promise a wonderful week.

Their second reaction, about five hours out, was grief, since they were both struck with serious cases of seasickness. They tried lying down, sitting up, walking, standing still—nothing relieved the condition.

While they were both standing at the rail, trying not to look at the waves beneath them, a friendly passenger approached and offered some advice.

"I know how you feel," he said, "but don't worry. No one ever died of seasickness."

"Please don't say that." Barbara said. "In my condition, dying is the only hopeful thing I have to look forward to."

A vacation is a period of travel during which you find that you took twice as many clothes and half as much money as you needed.

Anybody who says you can't take it with you never saw a car packed for a family vacation.

Willie had left the farm to spend a two-week vacation in the city. All his life, he'd heard stories about how rude city people could be. As a result, he'd been here three days and hadn't said a word to anyone but the check-in clerk at the hotel.

"This is silly," Willy thought. "How do I know all those stories are true? And even if they are, I'm man enough to deal with a little rudeness."

So he stood on a corner, waited for a prospect who didn't look very threatening, screwed up his courage, and approached a middle-aged man.

"Excuse me, sir," Willy said, "could you tell me what time it is, or should I just go to hell?"

• *Vulgarity* •

On the first day of school, the kindergarten teacher was distributing cookies and apple juice. When she reached little Stevie, he looked up at her and said, "I don't want any of your damn cookies."

Somewhat taken aback, the teacher said, "Now, Stevie, the proper way to say it is, 'No, thank you.'"

He looked her straight in the eye and said, "No damn cookies." Then he repeated it four or five times, before the teacher went back to her desk.

At the end of the day, the teacher left a message on the answering machine at Stevie's home that she wanted to meet with one of his parents. The next morning, his mother appeared.

"I offered Stevie cookies yesterday," she said, "and his response was 'I don't want any of your damn cookies.' Then he said, 'No damn cookies' several times."

Stevie's mother looked a little perplexed. Then she shrugged and said, "Screw him. If he doesn't want the goddamn things, don't give him any."

Because his truck was being repaired, the farmer drove his mules into town along a back road. He was gone a lot longer than his wife had expected, and when he finally returned, she asked him why he was so late.

"I picked up Reverend Hargrove on the way back," he said. "From there on, those mules didn't understand a thing I said."

• *War* •

The social studies teacher had just finished a unit on war and peace. "How many of you," he asked, "would say you're opposed to war?"

Not surprisingly, all hands went up. Then the teacher asked, "Who'll give us a reason for being opposed to war?"

A large, bored-looking boy in the back of the room raised his hand.

"Moose?" the teacher said.

"I hate war," Moose said, "because wars make history, and I hate history."

War does not determine who is right—only who is left.

· X-Y-Z ·

→ *These last three letters of the alphabet don't offer many possibilities. It isn't easy to come up with jokes about such topics as xylophones, yachts, or zippers. So, we've decided to use this end of the alphabet for some miscellaneous jokes that don't fit under any of the earlier topics.*

. . .

A man is lost in a desert, moving along very slowly, barely able to stay on his feet. Suddenly, at the top of a hill, a guy on a camel appears, with 20 or 30 ties draped over his arm.

"Water!" the first man cries.

"I don't have any water," the guy on the camel says. "But I can sell you a nice tie for $15."

"I don't want a tie! I want water."

"Okay, two for $25."

"No ties! Just tell me where I can find some water!"

"Oh, all right. Go in this direction, where I just came from. In a straight line from here, you'll see a small palm tree. About 50 yards past the tree, you'll get your water."

The camel gallops off, the man follows the directions, and he finds himself facing a young man.

"Water!" he says hoarsely. "Do you have water?"

"Plenty of water here," the young man says.

"Thank goodness! Let me have some."

"Sorry, sir," the young man says. "We don't serve anyone not wearing a tie."

The barbershops were separated by only one block, so they were constantly competing with each other for customers. One day, a new sign went up in the window of one of the shops. It read, "Haircuts Now $4.00."

An hour later, the other shop displayed a larger sign saying, "We repair $4.00 haircuts."

Surrounded by his children, grandchildren, and great-grandchildren, the octogenarian was holding court. "Don't think of me as an old man," he whined. "I'm healthy, everything is fine. My heart's still pumping away, my liver is strong, and my mind, knock wood . . . Who is it?"

This one takes place in a bar on the top floor of the tallest building in the city. A guy who's obviously had too much to drink says to another patron, "How would you like to make a little bet?"

"What do you want to bet on?" the man asks.

"I'll bet you," the drunk says, "that I can jump out that window over there and come back inside within five seconds."

"That's ridiculous," the man says.

"If you're so sure," the drunk says nastily, "put your money up."

"All right, I will," the man says.

He and the drunk each give a hundred dollars to the bartender. The drunk goes to the window and jumps out. A few seconds later, he hops back in, takes the money from the bartender, and gulps down a drink."

The man goes to the window and looks out. No platform, no net, nothing that could have stopped the drunk from plummeting to the ground.

"Unbelievable!" he says. "Well, if you can do it, so can I! Double or nothing, I can do what you just did."

"You're on!" the drunk says, and they each give the bartender $200. The man leaps out the window and falls to the ground below.

The bartender hands the money to the grinning drunk and says, "You know, Superman, sometimes you can be really offensive."

To err is human, but to blame someone else is even more human.

Two grandmothers, old friends who hadn't seen each other for several years, sat sipping tea. "I'm so proud of my grandson," one of them said. "Next week, he graduates from law school."

"NYU?" the second asked.

"And why not me?" the first one responded.

. . .

A famous abstract artist, suffering from severe vision problems, underwent surgery that proved to be remarkably successful. He was so grateful that he gave the doctor a gift—a painting he identified as *Eye*.

When a friend of the surgeon came to see the painting, he was stunned by the sight. The weird shapes and hideous colors were almost too disturbing for him to bear.

"So, what do you think?" the eye surgeon asked.

His friend replied, "Be grateful you aren't a proctologist."

"How far do you live from your office?" the doctor asked.

"A little over a mile," Harrison said.

"And can you shower when you get to work?"

"Sure," Harrison said. "We have a small gym for the executives."

"Good," the doctor said. "I'm going to prescribe some daily exercise for you. I want you to jog to and from work every day. And while you're jogging, I want you to roll a hula hoop along with you."

Harrison's first reaction was disbelief. But the doctor assured him the exercise would work wonders for him, both physically and mentally.

After a month of the daily exercise, Harrison felt like a new man. He now looked forward to what originally had sounded impossible to him.

But one evening, he arrived at the garage where he stored his hoop and was told that it had been stolen during the day.

When the manager saw the distraught look on his face, he said, "Don't worry, Mr. Harrison. We'll pay for the hoop."

"Pay for it?" Harrison screamed. "You bet you'll pay for it! But what good will that do? How am I going to get home tonight?"

Orrin, a comedy writer of some esteem, invited his friend Blanche to a comedy convention. Their first stop was a large auditorium filled with hundreds of joke writers. They took seats in the back to watch the proceedings.

One member of the audience went up to the stage, stood in front of the microphone, and said, "11."

The audience burst out laughing.

A second audience member went up and said, "604." Loud laughter.

After six or seven people had done this and gotten the same audience reaction, Blanche said, "What's going on here, Orrin?"

"These are all joke writers," Orrin explained. "They know just about every joke ever written, and they have them numbered. When they hear the number, they think of the joke and laugh."

"Fascinating," Blanche said. "Can anybody go up on that stage?"

"I don't see why not," Orrin said.

So Blanche made her way down the aisle and up onto the stage. She stood in front of the microphone and, with a big grin, said, "401."

Dead silence. She repeated the number. More silence. Humiliated, she rushed off the stage and back to her seat.

"What happened?" she whispered to Orrin.

"I should have warned you," Orrin said. "Ethnic jokes never go over big with this crowd."

Fred wasn't much of a drinker, so when he came home drunk one evening, Heather was astonished. "I can't believe this!" she said. "Your eyes! They're all bloodshot!"

He said, "If you think they look bad from there, you should see them from the inside."

. . .

On her way from one store to another in the mall, Pam spotted an old friend. "Sam!" she called out. "Sam! Over here."

When he realized who was calling him, Sam slowly made his way over to her.

"Sam!" she said. "I haven't seen you in—what, it must be nearly a year."

"I guess so," Sam said quietly.

"But what's the matter?" Pam asked. "You don't look very good. In fact, you look terrible."

"Well," Sam said, "about a month ago, an uncle of mine died and left me $10,000."

"Really?" Pam said, not sure whether to offer condolences or congratulations.

"And then, two weeks ago, I learned that a distant cousin had died, and he left me $50,000."

"But why do you look—"

"And last week, I found out that I've inherited nearly a million dollars from the estate of my great-grandfather."

"I see," said Pam. "But with all this good news, why are you looking so glum?"

"This week," Sam said, "not a penny!"

If a man talks to himself in a forest with no woman around to hear him, is he still wrong?

. . .

During the Senate impeachment trial of President Clinton, the *New York Times* printed a letter from an observer in Australia. "Thank God," he wrote, "we got the convicts and you got the Puritans."

On a cross-country driving trip, the guys decided to take a tour of the brewery of their favorite beer. As they marveled at the process, one of them slipped and fell into a huge vat of beer. While his friends waited outside, brewery workers tried to save him.

A half hour later, one of the supervisors came out to tell the guys their friend had drowned.

"Do you think he suffered much?" one of the guys asked.

"I don't think so," the supervisor said. "In fact, before he drowned, he climbed out three times to go to the bathroom."

"Give me a double scotch," the man said. The bartender served him, and he drank it down in a single gulp. Then he peeked into his shirt pocket.

"Another double," he said. He drank it and again looked into his pocket.

After a third double shot, he did the same

thing. By now the bartender was burning with curiosity.

"Why do you keep looking in your pocket after each drink?" he asked.

"I have a picture of my wife in there," he said. "When she starts to look good, I know it's time to stop drinking."

Jake stopped to pick up Willy, his carpool partner. Willy climbed into the car and stared straight ahead, without saying a word.

"Did you wake up grouchy this morning?" Jake asked.

"No!" Willy barked. "Let her wake up by herself!"

When Dom returned from his honeymoon, his father-in-law said, "I'm glad to have you for a son-in-law, Dom. To show you how glad, I'm going to make you a half-partner in my business."

"Well, thank you."

"You can be in charge of the factory."

"Oh, no, I couldn't do that. I hate factories. All that noise and dirt."

"Oh? Well, then, you can run the office."

"No, I'm afraid not. I hate office work. Cooped up behind a desk all day? No good."

Exasperated, the old man said, "I've just given you half my business, and you tell me you won't work in the factory or the office! What do you want?"

"Well," Dom said, "would you consider buying me out?"

Mabel and Lou had been married 50 years, and they still managed to get along pretty well. One afternoon, having just returned from a walk, they sat on the couch to relax. After a few minutes, Lou stood up, headed for the kitchen, and said, "I'm going to have some seltzer."

"Please bring me a glass, too," Mabel said.

"Okay."

"Maybe you should write it down," she said. "You know how easily you forget things."

"I won't forget."

"Put a slice of lemon in it," Mabel said. "Do you want to write that down?"

"I'll remember," he said.

"Can I have a few pretzels, too?" Mabel asked. "And maybe you do want to write all this down."

"I don't have to write it down," Lou said. "You want a glass of seltzer with a slice of lemon and some pretzels on the side."

"Very good," Mabel said, and she went back to reading her magazine.

Lou was gone quite a while. When he returned, he held out a plate to Mabel. It had two fried eggs on it.

Mabel said, "Took you a long time. And you forgot my rye toast."

A man staggered out of a bar, having had far too much to drink. As he weaved his way down the sidewalk, he encountered two delivery men hauling a grandfather clock from a truck. He lost his footing, bumped into one of the delivery men, and knocked the clock to the ground.

"You clumsy fool!" one of the delivery men said. "Look what you've done!"

"Sorry," the drunk said. "But why can't you guys wear wristwatches like everybody else?"

It was one of those Minnesota winters, 40° below 0, with a wind-chill factor off the scale. Pat braved this weather to get to his favorite spot in the world—his neighborhood bar. He ordered a drink and told the bartender to put it on his tab.

"Can't do that," the bartender said. "You owe us a pretty hefty sum already."

"Come on," Pat said. "I'll be able to pay the whole bill next week."

"Okay," the bartender said. "I'll give you the

drink. And I'll write what you owe me right here on the wall."

"Don't do that," Pat said. "I don't want everybody to see that."

"Don't worry," the bartender said. "I'll just hang your coat over it—till you pay the bill."

A grandmother held her little grandson's hand as they walked along the shore. Without warning, a huge wave rose above them, knocked the woman down, and washed the boy away from the shore.

Nearly hysterical, the woman fell to her knees and cried to the heavens, "Lord, save my grandson! Don't let anything happen to him! Please return him to me! I beg you, Lord, send my grandson back!"

At that instant, another wave rose above her and deposited the boy at her feet. Some water spouted out of his mouth, and he smiled at her.

The woman looked up at the sky and said, "He had a hat!"

■ ■ ■

PART THREE

A Horse Walks into a Bar . . .

▲

That's enough of the real world for a while. Let's enter the realm of the talking animal. For some reason, jokes about talking animals almost always seem to be set in bars. We'll leave it to you to think of some possible reasons for that.

In a few of these jokes, the animals don't actually talk, but they do play a major role in the plot. One or two of the jokes don't even involve animals at all. But they all have the same surreal flavor to them.

In any case, these stories take place in or near one of the most interesting bars you're ever likely to come across.

▼

A grasshopper ambles into a bar, hops onto a stool, and says to the bartender, "I'll have a cold beer."

The bartender draws a beer, serves it to the grasshopper, and says, "You know, we serve a drink named after you."

The grasshopper wipes the foam from his lips and says, "Why would anybody name a drink Murray?"

A man walks into a bar and orders two shots of rye. He drinks one and slowly pours the other into the side pocket of his jacket.

"What the heck are you doing?" the bartender asks.

"It's for my pet mouse," the man says. "He likes rye whiskey as much as I do."

"Hey," the bartender says, "we don't serve weirdos in here. Get out!"

"I will not!" the man says. "My mouse and I want another round."

"No more for you, pal! Get out!"

"This is outrageous!" the man says. "I want to see your boss. Go get the manager."

From the man's pocket, a high-pitched voice adds, "Yeah! And tell him to bring his stupid cat with him!"

A skeleton walks into a bar and says, "Give me a beer. And give me a mop."

Two ropes walk into a bar and order drinks. The bartender looks them up and down and says with a sneer, "We don't serve ropes. Get out. We don't want your kind in here."

Out on the sidewalk, one rope says to the other, "That bartender thinks he's so tough. Well, I'll show him!"

"Let's just get out of here," the second rope says.

"No!" the first rope insists. "I'm going to get him to serve me a drink."

So the first rope twists his body until it forms a huge knot. Then he messes up his ends and goes back into the bar.

"I'll have a whiskey sour," he says.

The bartender looks him over and says, "Say, you're a rope, aren't you?"

"No," the rope says. "I'm a frayed knot."

A snail shows up at the door of a bar. The bartender sees it, picks it up, and tosses it into the street. Six months later, the snail reappears in the doorway.

"What the hell was that for?" it yells.

A belligerent dog limps into a bar and snarls. All conversation stops, and the frightened customers stare at the dog. The dog limps a few steps farther in and growls, "I'm looking for the man who shot my paw!"

Two friends walk into a bar, Barney leading a German shepherd, Alfred with a Chihuahua. The bartender immediately calls out, "No dogs allowed. Out!"

Standing across the street from the bar, the two think over their situation.

"Guess we better find another place," says Alfred.

"Not on your life," Barney retorts. "The bartenders here change shifts in 20 minutes. And I know how to get the new guy to let us in."

Twenty minutes later, the early bartender leaves and heads for home. Barney puts on a pair of dark glasses and takes the German shepherd into the bar.

"No dogs—" the new bartender begins, but Barney cuts him off.

"Seeing-eye dog," he says.

Waiting outside, Alfred sees that Barney's plan worked. He puts on a pair of dark glasses and goes inside with his dog.

"Seeing-eye dog," he says to the bartender.

"You have a Chihuahua for a seeing-eye dog?" the bartender asks skeptically.

Thinking fast, Alfred says, "They gave me a Chihuahua?"

A duck goes into a drugstore next to the bar and says, "Give me some Chapstick. And put it on my bill."

The same duck walks into a bar and says to the bartender, "Got any duck food?"

The bartender looks down at him, annoyed, and says, "This is a bar. We don't sell duck food."

An hour later, the duck is back. "Got any duck food?" he asks.

"Look, you," the bartender says, "I told you before, we don't sell duck food here. Now get out!"

Twenty minutes later, the duck comes in again and says, "Got any duck food?"

"All right, buddy," the bartender says, "now listen to me! This is a bar. We don't sell duck food. And if you come in and ask for duck food again, I'm going to nail your feet to the floor! Got it? Good! Get out!"

The duck leaves. An hour later, he comes back in. "Got any nails?" he asks.

"No!" the bartender screams.

"Good," the duck says. "Got any duck food?"

Guy walks up to a bar and orders a beer. While the bartender is getting the drink, the guy hears a tiny voice say, "Nice suit."

He looks around, but no one is nearby. Then he hears the same voice say, "I really like that tie."

Again, he looks around. Again, no one. Then the voice says, "Good haircut. You must have a terrific barber."

The bartender returns with the beer, and the guy says, "I keep hearing someone talking."

"Saying nice things about you?" the bartender asks.

"Yeah."

"Those are our peanuts. They're complimentary."

A man goes into a bar that has a piano player, who has a pet monkey sitting on his piano. The man orders a drink, takes a sip, and turns to listen to the music. The monkey comes up behind him and spits into his drink.

"Hey!" the man says to the piano player, "Do you know your monkey just spit in my drink?"

"No," the musician says, "but if you hum a few bars, I can probably pick it up."

A kangaroo hops into a bar, sits on a stool, and orders a Singapore sling. The bartender, who's been well-trained in not embarrassing customers, suppresses his surprise and goes off to mix the drink.

He returns with the Singapore sling, slips a napkin under the glass, and says, "That'll be $11.50." The kangaroo looks up at him, takes a $20 out of its pouch, and lays it on the bar.

While he's ringing up the charge and counting out the change, the bartender thinks, "What harm could it do? I'll be polite, and I won't embarrass him."

He returns and puts the change on the counter. After a pause, he says, "You know, we haven't had many kangaroos in here."

The kangaroo sips its drink, puts the glass down on the bar, and says, "And at $11.50 a drink, you're not likely to get many more."

A man walks into a bar pulling a mangy dog on a leash. The bartender says, "No dogs allowed! Get him out of here!"

"Wait," the man says. "This is a talking dog."

"Who do you think you're kidding?" the bartender says. "Get the dog out of here!"

"No, no!" the man says. "This dog really can talk."

The bartender hesitates, then says, "If the dog talks, you can both stay. But if he can't, you give me a hundred bucks and get out."

"It's a deal," the man says. Then he turns to the dog.

"Chips," he says, "what's on the top of a house?"

The dog responds with something that sounds a lot like "Roof!"

The man says, "And how would you describe the surface of sandpaper?"

The dog's response could be taken for "Rough!"

"Good," the man says. "Now, who's the greatest home run hitter who ever lived?"

"Ruth!" the dog barks.

The bartender grabs the man by the back of his collar, throws him out on the sidewalk, and says, "And don't come back until you're ready to pay me my hundred bucks!"

The bartender goes back inside, the man brushes himself off, and the dog says, "Sorry. I guess I should have said 'Hank Aaron.'"

The next week, that same guy comes into the bar with another dog. "This one really talks," he tells the bartender. "And I'm looking to sell him for 50 bucks."

"Now, look," the bartender says, "I'm not—"

"Please, sir," the dog says, "won't you consider buying me? This man almost never feeds me, never plays with me or lets me run around, never shows me any affection. At one time in my life, I was a prized show dog, and I was even in several movies."

"Good Lord!" the bartender says, "The dog really does talk! Why are you willing to sell him so cheap?"

"Because," says the owner, "I can't stand listening to all his lies."

A man walks into a bar with a pig under his arm. The bartender looks them over and says, "How can you travel around with something so disgusting?"

The man indignantly says, "What kind of remark is that to make about my pet?"

The bartender says, "I was talking to the pig."

The football play-off game pitted the little animals against the big animals. (The game was being played only a block away from the bar.) The squirrels, raccoons, cats, and dogs were convinced that their speed and agility could defeat the likes of the hippo, the rhino, and the elephant. In spite of this confidence, however, the big animals led 41–0 at halftime.

During the break, the rabbit gave a stirring pep talk. Still, no one expected things to change in the second half.

Play began with the rabbit kicking off to the

big animals. The elephant caught the ball and began galumphing in the direction of the goal posts. But he was tripped up before he reached midfield.

In the huddle, the rabbit said, "Great play! Who stopped the elephant?"

"I did," the centipede said.

On the next play, the rhino was stopped behind the line of scrimmage. Back in the huddle, the rabbit asked, "Who tackled the rhino?"

"I did," the centipede answered.

On the next play, the centipede threw the hippo for a 15-yard loss. When the little animals returned to the huddle, the rabbit said to the centipede, "Great plays! Where were you during the first half?"

"I was in the locker room," the centipede said, "taping my ankles."

Two goats are standing outside a bar, when one of them uncovers a reel of film in a garbage can. They cooperate in getting the top off the reel, then devour all the film in the can.

"That was pretty good," one goat says.

"It was all right," the second one says. "But I liked the book better."

. . .

In a movie theater next to that same bar, a woman took a seat and noticed that the man in front of her was sitting next to a large dog. After the film began, the man would occassionally lean over and say something to the dog. In response, the dog would nod.

Not only that, but the funny scenes elicited from the dog something that sounded very much like laughter. And at the sad ending, the dog was whimpering.

The woman leaned forward and said, "Excuse me, sir, but I can't get over your dog's behavior."

"Frankly," the man said, "neither can I. He hated the book."

A man walks into a bar with a goose perched on his head. The bartender, who prides himself on being able to deal with any situation, calmly asks, "Can I help you?"

"You sure can," the goose says. "Get this guy out from under me!"

. . .

Guy comes into a bar with a pit bull on a leash. "Before you say anything," the guy says, "let the dog sit at the piano. He knows how to play a Bach cantata."

"Listen," the bartender says angrily, "I don't have time for—"

"I'd advise you to let him play," the guy says. "Once he sees a piano, he has to play or he attacks."

After only a slight hesitation, the bartender agrees. The dog hops onto the piano stool and starts playing. And he's awful.

When the dog is finished, the bartender says, "I should have let him attack. I'm sure his Bach is worse than his bite."

■ ■ ■

PART FOUR

Let Me Entertain You

▲

*Think about entertainers. They claim that all they
want to do is make us happy. Well, this section has
a similar goal; all it's meant to do is make you
laugh. But since the butt of these jokes is entertainers themselves, they might protest that this isn't exactly what they had in mind.*

*By the way, we've included not only actors,
singers, etc. in this chapter, but also politicians. If
you have reservations about politics being treated as
a form of show biz, skip to the next chapter.*

▼

⋅ *Actors* ⋅

For two years, Wilson had been knocking on producers' doors, going to auditions, and more or less begging for work. He had no luck at all, until one day he auditioned for the role of Marc Antony in *Julius Caesar.* Although he didn't get the part, he was hired to play a citizen of Rome in three crowd scenes.

"Mom!" he said excitedly into the phone, "I got an acting job! I've actually landed a part in a play."

"That's wonderful!" his mother said. "What is the play about?"

"Well," he began, "it's about this ordinary Roman citizen. . . ."

At the cemetery, the coffin containing the wife of the famous actor was being lowered into the ground. The actor had to be restrained from throwing himself onto the coffin.

Later, over coffee, his friend said, "You really broke down there at the last minute."

"That was nothing," the actor said. "You should have seen me at the funeral home."

A traveling theater company was apparently suffering from bad word-of-mouth. As they prepared for their final performance in town, one of the actors asked the stage manager how things looked in the audience.

"Looks better than last night," the stage manager said. "But don't worry, the cast still has them outnumbered."

The acerbic movie critic found himself sharing the couch on a talk show with Lance Handsome, a movie star with an ego the size of North Dakota.

"Would you believe it?" Lance said to the host. "My parents didn't even want me to become an actor!"

The critic leaned into camera range and said, "I saw your last movie. They got their wish."

The star of the play had been moping backstage for hours after the play ended. One stagehand asked, "What's the matter with her? She was handed six bouquets of flowers during her curtain calls."

"I saw the florist's bill," the second stagehand said. "She paid for eight."

Interviewer: So you moved from Broadway to Hollywood in hopes of furthering your career. Did you gain anything by the move?
Actor: Three hours. But even that was good only for the first day.

On reading .the will of a famous actor, his lawyer reported that the actor wanted to be cremated and have ten percent of his ashes thrown in his agent's face.

A has-been actor answered a call from his agent, who said he had an offer of a walk-on part in a movie. "The part consists of three spoken lines," the agent said.

"Three lines!" the actor shouted. "I won't do it! The offer is an insult. Why, a part like that would ruin my reputation."

"I know," the agent said, "and this might be your last chance to accomplish that."

"Sir," the actor said, "I would like permission to marry your daughter."

"Forget it," the father said. "Never in my wildest dreams would I let my daughter marry an actor."

"Before you make a final decision, sir, would you be willing to come and see me perform?"

"Sure."

So the father and his daughter went to see the play the young man was appearing in. When the play was over, they went backstage to his dressing room.

"Okay," the father said, "you can marry her. You're no actor."

Two guys sitting at a bar are sort of eavesdropping on a conversation between two other guys. The conversation is about international politics, technology, and even a little philosophy.

"This has been really interesting," one of them says. "It's a pleasure to meet someone so smart. Do you know what your IQ is?"

"Sure," the other says. "It's 150. What's yours?"

"About 145," the second guy says. Then the two of them leave.

The other two guys sit there staring into their beers. "Did you hear that?" one asks.

"Yeah," the other says. "Do you know what your IQ is?"

"About 75. Yours?"

"About the same. Are you Broadway or Hollywood?"

Jackie Coogan was one of the most popular child film actors of the 1930s (though more people probably remember him for the role he played decades later on TV—Uncle Fester in *The Addams Family*). In one of the movies he made as a kid, he was supposed to break into tears when another character told him his mother had just died. In take after take, Jackie couldn't make the tears come.

The director suggested he imagine that his own mother was really dead. He tried that, but still no tears. Finally, he said to the director, "Would it be all right if I imagined that my dog died?"

Ego? I know an actor who takes along a makeup man when he goes for passport photos.

. . .

Then there's the story about the actor who fell off a cruise ship as it passed a lighthouse. He drowned after swimming in circles for hours. He just refused to let that spotlight get away from him.

The performance of *Hamlet* ended at 11:00, and the cast nervously milled about at the restaurant, waiting for the early edition of the next morning's paper. At 1:30, someone came running in with the review.

Davidson grabbed the paper from him, flipped to the theater review, and read aloud, "Last night, Richard Davidson played Hamlet. Hamlet lost."

• *Athletes* •

"Coach," the interviewer said, "to what do you attribute your success at selecting young players?"

"I have a system," the coach answered. "I take all the recruits into the woods. When I fire my gun, they all start running. The ones who run around the trees become my guards. The ones who run into the trees become tackles."

One of the big football colleges has decided to expand to three squads next year. One squad will play offense, one will play defense, and the third will attend classes.

During a TV debate, sports columnist Bob Hatch listed a series of abuses that made a mockery of the word student in the term student-athlete.

His opponent, Coach Winkler, angrily retorted, "Frankly, I'm sick and tired of hearing all these rumors about college athletes. It just so happens that a recent study showed that a majority of student-athletes are making straight A's."

"I read that study," Hatch said. "What I want to know is, when are those guys going to learn to write the rest of the alphabet?"

Coach Winkler was watching a dismal practice performance when one of his scouts approached him, accompanied by a husky teenager.

"Coach," he said, "I want you to meet a kid who's good enough to play on your team."

"I've got plenty of kids good enough to play on

my team," the coach said. "What I need is somebody good enough to play for Notre Dame."

"Honey, why don't you and Van play golf together anymore?"

"Would you play with a guy who cheats on his scorecard and moves the ball when you aren't looking?"

"Certainly not."

"Well, neither will Van."

A diplomat from a distant country was treated by the president's staff to a Washington Redskins game. He watched intently, but without comment, during the first half. During halftime, his host asked him how he was enjoying the game.

"It's very interesting," the diplomat said, "but it seems like a great deal of fuss over 25 cents."

"25 cents?" his host said. "What do you mean?"

"These people around us," the diplomat said, "keep shouting 'Get the quarter back!' "

While watching his first football game, a different diplomat found himself impatient with all the huddling. He told his companion, "It's not a bad game, but there are just too many committee meetings."

Warren's first attempt at skydiving was so exhilarating that he went up again the next day. He felt a lot more confident this time, having touched ground without incident the day before.

When he received the signal, he leaped from the plane and luxuriated in the pleasure of the free-fall. At the proper moment, he pulled the rip-cord and waited for the parachute to open. Nothing happened.

Warren stayed cool. He pulled the cord for the emergency chute. Nothing happened.

Now he was no longer cool. Near panic, he looked down and saw another man flying up from the ground beneath them. As they passed each other, Warren yelled, "Do you know anything about parachutes?"

"No!" the other guy yelled. "Do you know anything about gas stoves?"

Lenny and Rob arrived at the first tee. Lenny teed up, hit a mighty shot, then watched the ball sail to the green and roll in for a hole-in-one.

Rob put his ball on the tee. Then he said,

"Okay, now I'll take my practice swing. Then we can start the game."

What's the difference between golf and politics? In golf, you can't improve your lie.

The manager walked out to the mound and said to the rookie pitcher, "Son, I think you've had enough."

The kid protested, "But I struck this guy out the last time he came up."

"I know," the manager said, taking the ball from him, "but we're still in the same inning."

While watching a football game with his five-year-old son, Willie exploded. "Look at that guy!" he fumed. "Every time he gets the ball, he fumbles! Why would they keep an incompetent like that on the field?"

"Daddy?" the kid said tentatively. "Maybe it's his ball."

. . .

The practice preceding the big game was one of the most depressing things the coach had ever seen. Since it was too late to make any real changes, he thought a strong dose of sarcasm might help.

"All right, men," he said to the team in the locker room. "From where I stand, things don't look good. I think it's time to go back to fundamentals."

He bent down and picked up a ball. "Now, this," he said, "is a football. When you're about to throw it . . ."

"Wait, wait, wait, Coach!" one of the tackles cried out. "Not so fast!"

The interviewer asked the manager to describe his idea of a dream player for a baseball team.

"He'd be a player," the manager said, "who plays every position perfectly, never makes an error, and never strikes out. The trouble is, I can never get that guy to put down his beer and come down to the field."

Golfer: I'd move heaven and earth to be able to break a hundred!

Caddy: You'd better get to work on heaven.

You've already moved enough earth to build a railroad.

Golfer: I want you to know that this is not the game I usually play.

Caddy: I should hope not, sir. And what game do you usually play?

The boxer marched into his manager's office, closed the door for privacy, and put on his most determined look.

"Now, listen," he said to his manager, "The time has come. I'm in the best shape I've ever been in. I've been training for six months. I've stayed away from desserts, I haven't been drinking, I've been getting to bed by ten o'clock every night. I've never been in better shape. And I want Killer McPug! Get me a fight with Killer McPug!"

The manager stood up, walked from his desk, and put his arm around his boxer's shoulders. "If I've told you once," he said calmly, "I've told you a hundred times—you are Killer McPug."

. . .

The golf pro dragged himself into the clubhouse looking as though he'd just escaped a tornado.

"What's wrong?" a woman asked.

"I just lost a game to Houlihan," the pro said.

"What? But Houlihan's the worst player I've ever seen. How could he have beaten you?"

"He tricked me," the pro said. "On the first tee, he asked for a handicap. I told him he could have 30, 40, 50 strokes—any handicap he wanted. He said, 'Just give me two gotchas.' "

"What's a gotcha?" the woman asked.

"That's what I wanted to know," the pro said. "Houlihan said, 'You'll see.' Then, as I was teeing off, just as I had my club poised, he yelled out 'Gotcha!' "

"I can guess what happened," the woman said.

"Sure," the pro said. "The scream threw me off, and I missed the ball completely."

"Understandable," the woman said. "But still, that's only one swing. How did he win the game?"

The pro answered, "You try swinging at a golf ball while waiting for that second 'gotcha!' "

"I thought I told you to keep an eye on your cousin," the mother said. "Where is he?"

"Well," her son said thoughtfully, "if he knows as much about canoeing as he thinks he does,

he's out canoeing. If he knows as little as I think
he does, he's out swimming."

It was a happy marriage, in spite of their not-quite-
compatible interests. He was mad about golf. She
spent all her free time at antique auctions.

Once, in the middle of the night, he cried out in
his sleep, "Fore!"

Fast asleep, she immediately responded, "Four-
fifty!"

As Thompson prepared to tee off, a woman in a
wedding gown came running across the green.
She grabbed him by the arm and began tugging
him toward the clubhouse.

"Hold on just a minute!" he said, pulling himself
free. "I said only if it rains!"

In a desperate attempt to lose weight, Carter took
up tennis. After a few outings, he was telling his
friend about the ordeal.

"My brain gives the commands: Stretch out for
that serve! Charge the net! Use your whole body
for this swing! Race back into position!"

"And what happens?" his friend asked.

"My body says, 'Are you talking to me?' "

. . .

"Say, caddy, why do you keep looking at your watch?"

"It isn't a watch, sir. It's a compass."

After the wrestling match, the interviewer approached Bruiser in his locker room. "What happened out there tonight, Bruiser? Just about everyone expected you to win this match."

"I can't understand it," Bruiser said. "I won the rehearsal."

Jasper was a little nervous about his first attempt at skiing. His condition wasn't helped any when he arrived at the ski lodge. The registration form asked for his name, address, and HMO.

By the time Ted arrived at the football game, the first quarter was almost over. "Why are you so late?" his friend asked.

"I had to toss a coin to decide between going to church and coming to the game."

"How long could that have taken you?"

"Well, I had to toss it 14 times."

. . .

"Did you hear that Turnbull knocked a burglar unconscious in his house last night?"

"No kidding? How'd he do it?"

"With a four-iron."

"Really? How many strokes?"

A young woman, looking worn and weary, got on a crowded bus with a pair of ice skates slung over her shoulder. As the bus started up, a man offered her his seat.

"No, thank you," she said. "I've been sitting most of the morning."

In baseball, if at first you don't succeed, try playing second, shortstop, left field. . . .

"Closing time!" the playground supervisor called out. "Let's go, kids, time to go home for dinner!"

"All right!" one kid cried. "We win!"

"What do you mean, you win?" a kid from the opposing team said. "The score's nothing-nothing!"

"Yeah," the first kid said, "but we scored the first nothing."

. . .

Although Sam never passed up a chance to watch a baseball game, when his wife saw him sleeping in his favorite chair, she decided not to wake him. She figured his baseball clock would wake him in time for the game, and she went shopping.

When she returned three hours later, the TV was off, and he was still asleep. Shaking his shoulder gently, she said, "Honey, wake up. It's ten to four."

"Who's winning?" he asked.

It was a conference title game, and the sportscaster had mentioned several times that the place had been sold out long before game time. As he called the play-by-play, however, he kept noticing a single empty seat directly below his booth.

The empty seat was bothering him, so he sent an assistant downstairs to find out what was going on.

"Pardon me, sir," the assistant said to the man sitting next to the seat. "Do you happen to know why this seat is empty?"

"Yeah. It's my wife's seat."

"And why is it empty?"

"She died."

"Oh. I'm very sorry to hear that. But couldn't

you get a friend to come to the game with you today?"

"Impossible," the man said. "They're all at her funeral."

Dr. Drew had just joined the practice, and he often asked the older Dr. Mantel for advice. "This patient really has me baffled," Dr. Drew said. "Can't sleep at night, has constant headaches, and often feels nauseous. I don't know what to tell him."

"In a case like that," Dr. Mantel said, "you might do what I do. If the patient plays golf, tell him to stop. If he doesn't play golf, tell him to start."

If you watch a game, it's fun. If you play it, it's recreation. If you work at it, it's probably tennis.

If they keep tightening restrictions on alcohol at stadiums, there's no telling what harm they may do. For some fans, the major attraction at a football game is the extra pint after a touchdown.

. . .

The manager came storming out of the dugout to protest an infield-fly-rule call by the umpire. "What kind of call was that?" he demanded. "Do you need somebody to explain the rules to you?"

"I've got my rule book right here," the umpire said quietly, taking the book out of his back pocket.

"If it's yours," the manager sputtered, "it must be written in Braille."

"My doctor tells me I can't play tennis."

"So, she's played with you, too?"

Hank and Frank had both become millionaires overnight when they sold their Internet business. They decided to begin living like the rich men they now were. Their first foray into rich-man's-land would be golf.

After joining a country club, they went straight to a golf shop and bought everything—pants, shoes, shirts, hats, clubs, bags, balls. Fully equipped, they returned to the country club.

"Sorry, gentlemen," the starter said, "but you can't play today."

"Why not?" Hank asked.

"We have no caddies today."

Hank and Frank looked at each other, puzzled. "That's OK," Frank said. "Just for today, we'll settle for a BMW."

The scrawny kid had made the football team because he was a terrific runner. But the coach was reluctant to send him in to tussle with all those brawny players. In the last game of the season, with less than a minute to play, the coach called his name.

Elated, the kid threw off his warmup jacket and trotted to the coach's end of the bench. He hopped from foot to foot, waiting for the coach's instructions.

"We're out of time-outs," the coach said. "Go in there and get hurt."

"Is this a good stream for fish?"

"Must be. I haven't been able to coax a single one out of it yet."

Melinda was expecting Sam home for dinner at 5:30. Here it was 7:00, and no word from Sam. Forty-five minutes later, he arrived home, looking as though he'd been through a terrible ordeal.

"Sam!" Melinda cried. "What happened? You look awful."

"We were playing golf," Sam said, dropping onto the sofa. "And the boss had a heart attack on the third hole. Died instantly."

"Oh, that must have been horrible!" Melinda said.

"It was," Sam said. "For fifteen more holes, it was hit the ball, drag the boss, hit the ball, drag the boss. . . ."

During the season, Coach Rudnik treated his players like recruits in boot camp. When he heard that two of his running backs were slipping out for drinks late at night, he decided to put a stop to it.

The night before an out-of-town game, Coach checked their hotel room shortly after midnight and found them missing. He went straight to the bar in the hotel lobby. As he entered, he saw the two running backs slip into the men's room.

"What'll you have?" the bartender asked.

"Club soda," Coach said. "And while you're at it, see what the backs in the boys' room will have."

Two brothers played golf together regularly, but they really couldn't stand each other. While teeing up, one brother said, "Will you please stop that infernal humming! You're going to drive me out of my mind!"

The second brother said, "That would be less like a drive than a short putt."

"When I was in college, I was almost single-handedly responsible for Ohio State beating Michigan three years in a row."

"Really? Which team were you on?"

• *Musicians* •

Irv and Merv had played jazz together for most of their 80 years. When Irv was ready to check out, Merv asked him to come back and tell him what the afterlife was like.

One night as Merv was falling asleep, he heard Irv's voice calling him. "Irv!" he said. "Is it you?"

"It's me, man" Irv said cheerfully. "I just wanted to give you that report you asked for."

"Heaven?" Merv asked. "Are you in heaven?"

"You bet I am," Irv said. "And it's better than we could have hoped. I jam every day with Jelly Roll

Morton, Count Basie, Bird, and every other cat
we've been missing all these years."

"That's terrific!" Merv said.

"Yeah, well, mostly terrific," Irv responded.

"What do you mean mostly?"

"Well, like most things," Irv said, "there's good
news and there's bad news. The good news is that
all these cats play even better than they did before. The bad news is that St. Peter has this girl-
friend who sings."

Harkins, a jazz musician who wants to get away
from it all, arranges to spend two weeks at an island in the Indian Ocean that even his travel
agents have never heard of. As the boat nears the
shore, Harkins notices the constant sound of
drumming coming from the island.

He gets off the boat and sees a boy standing
near the water. He asks the boy how long the
drumming will go on. The boy looks about nervously and says in halting English, "Very bad
when drumming stops." Then he runs off.

At the end of the day, the drumming is still
going, and it is starting to get on Harkins's
nerves. So, he asks a woman when the drumming
will stop. She looks as if she's just been reminded
of something very unpleasant.

"Very bad when the drumming stops," she says, and hurries away.

Every time he asks about the drumming, he gets the same response. Two days later, Harkins can't stand the mystery anymore. He hunts down one of the island officials, corners him, and demands, "Tell me what happens when the drumming stops!"

The official looks troubled. He looks around in fear. Finally, he says, "Bass solo."

→ *Before reading the next batch of jokes, please see our disclaimer under UKULELES on page 82. Heaven knows that no one here has anything personally against any group of musicians. It's just that these jokes were too good to pass up.*

What do you call someone who spends most of his time with professional musicians?

A drummer.

How do you know when it's a drummer knocking at your door?

As you listen, the knock slows down.

. . .

What do you call a drummer with half a brain?
  Gifted.

What did the drummer get on his IQ test?
  Drool.

Why do jazz bands have bass players?
  To explain things to the drummer.

What's the difference between a drummer and a
drum machine?
  With a drum machine, you have to punch the
information in only once.

Why are orchestra intermissions limited to 20
minutes?
  So they don't have to retrain the drummer.

How does a trumpet player get away with parking
in a spot reserved for the handicapped?
  He leaves two drumsticks on the dashboard.

. . .

Did you hear about the drummer who got into college?
   No.
   Neither did I.

• *Opera* •

What's the difference between a wounded rhino and a soprano?
   Jewelry.

• *Politicians* •

Rawlings was taking his young son on a tour of the nation's capital. In the gallery of the House of Representatives, the boy pointed to a man standing in front of a lectern.
   "Dad," the boy asked, "who's that man?"

"He's the chaplain of the House," Rawlings answered.

"Does he pray for the people who work here?"

Rawlings thought for a few seconds. Then he said, "My guess is that after looking around at the people who work here, he prays for the country."

A newspaper reporter at the state capital sent an anonymous e-mail to every member of the state legislature. "Get out of town," it read. "The attorney general has found out everything." The legislative session was called off for lack of attendance.

A politician is someone who approaches every problem with an open mouth.

From Washington, D.C., down to the most local of aldermen, politicians help simplify the most complicated matters of history. If it happened while they were in office and it's good, they conceived it. If it's bad, they inherited it.

. . .

"Hey, I hear you're working at the mayor's office."

"Yep. I'm the deputy assistant to the undersecretary for developing issues."

"Wow! Sounds like a job that calls for a lot of know-how."

"Actually, it calls for a lot more know-who."

Like any president, William Howard Taft had to display a thick skin when attacked by his opponents. One day, his son said something to him that Mrs. Taft considered disrespectful.

"Aren't you going to punish him?" she asked.

"If he said it to me as his father, I will," Taft replied. "But if he was addressing the president of the United States, he was only exercising his constitutional privilege."

"Senator, about that speech you gave the other night—a lot of people in your state aren't clear about just where you stand on the issue."

"Good. It took three speech writers a week to write it just that way."

Sitting at a bar in the lobby of a Washington hotel, a political reporter known for his acid comments about the Washington crowd struck up a conversation with the man next to him. They talked about baseball, the weather, and a couple of current movies.

Then the reporter said, "I heard a really funny joke this morning. It seems the president and two of his aides—"

"Before you go any further," the other man said, "I should tell you I work at the White House."

"Oh," said the reporter. "Okay. The—President—and—two—of—his—aides. . . ."

A surgeon, an architect, and a politician were considering the question of whose profession was the oldest.

"I think my line of work would win this one hands down," the surgeon said. "After all, Eve was created from Adam's rib, and that sounds like surgery to me."

"Maybe," the architect said, "but before Adam, order was created out of chaos. That was an architectural accomplishment."

"Sure," the politician said. "But before that, someone had to create the chaos."

· · ·

During a televised question-and-answer session, Senator Burton was asked to identify the goal of legislation.

"The goal of legislation," he said, "is the greatest good for the greatest number."

His challenger immediately chimed in, saying, "The problem is that in the senator's mind, the greatest number is numero uno."

It was a bitter floor fight over new tax legislation, and the Speaker of the House used every means he could think of to gather the needed votes. He bargained, he cajoled, and he threatened.

Congresswoman Kaplan turned out to be one of the important swing votes. She'd begun as a fierce opponent of the bill, but after the Speaker talked with her, she ended up voting for it.

Out in the hall, one of the bill's supporters said to her, "I'm glad you finally saw the light on this one."

"I didn't see the light," she said. "I felt the heat!"

Two very old men sat on a park bench, looking out at the terrain. After a long silence, one of them emitted a long, deep sigh.

The other stood up and said, "If you're going to talk politics, I'm leaving."

Politics: the art of looking for problems, finding them everywhere, diagnosing them incorrectly, and applying inappropriate solutions.

On election eve, the candidate asked the reporter, "Did you hear my last speech?"
"I certainly hope so," the reporter replied.

"I'm pleased to hear my opponent describe himself as a self-made man. That certainly relieves God of a frightening responsibility."

"What do you think about the debate over tax cuts?"
"Well, there are two sides to every issue."
"Yeah, but this debate is a lot like a bass drum."
"How's that?"
"After you've listened to both sides, you haven't heard much."

. . .

"The mayor," the editorial said, "is our city's version of a foghorn. Not only does he make loud, annoying noises, but he also constantly calls attention to problems without doing a thing about them."

My uncle hasn't voted in 40 years. He says the only reason they have elections is to see which network's poll was accurate.

Running for president in 1952, Adlai E. Stevenson said, "If the Republicans stop telling lies about us, we'll stop telling the truth about them."

Congressman Watkins was speaking at a county fair in one of the more remote sections of his district, an area he seldom visited except just before elections. He was interrupted in mid-sentence by a cabbage thrown at the stage by someone in the crowd.

He bent down, picked it up, and said, "It appears that one of my opponents has lost his head."

. . .

Later in that same speech, Watkins said, "I have heard the voice of the people calling me to serve."

Someone in the rear of the crowd called out, "It was probably just an echo."

America is the Land of Promise—especially just before election day.

On one of the Sunday morning TV talk shows, the moderator referred to a certain senator as a politician.

The newspaper columnist interrupted. "I think he qualifies as a statesman," he said.

"And how would you explain the distinction?" the moderator asked.

"A politician," the columnist said, "is a hot-air machine with a wagging tongue."

"And a statesman?"

"A statesman," the columnist replied, "is a politician who has learned to hold his tongue."

On the other hand . . .

According to Harry Truman, "A politician is a man who understands government. . . . A statesman is a politician who's been dead 10 or 15 years."

Bonomo, running for reelection as mayor, was visiting every store on Main Street. He arrived at the deli when there were no customers.

"Can I count on your vote?" he asked the deli owner.

"Afraid not, mayor," the owner said. "I've already promised my vote to Aldrich."

"Well," Bonomo said with a wink, "in politics, promising and performing are two different matters."

"In that case," said the deli owner, "I'll be glad to give you my promise."

"Good morning, sir. Can I count on your vote in tomorrow's election?"

"Vote for you? Why I'd vote for the devil first!"

"I understand, sir. But since your brother isn't running, can I count on your vote?"

The campaign manager was going over some last-minute details in preparation for the televised de-

. . .

After the senator's rousing speech, one of her aides took her aside. "There were a couple of things in the speech I didn't understand," the aide said.

The senator replied, "Those were probably the topics that I referred to in a strong, confident way to keep from showing that I don't understand them either."

"Are you a member of any organized political party?"

"No. I'm a Republican."

Two opposing county chairmen were sharing a rare moment together. The Democratic chairman said, "I never pass up a chance to promote the party. For example, whenever I take a cab, I give the driver a sizable tip and say, 'Vote Democratic.'"

His opponent said, "I have a better scheme, and it doesn't cost me a nickel. I don't give any tip at all. And when I leave, I also say, 'Vote Democratic.'"

bate. "Now, you're sure you know the words and phrases we gave you for each issue?" he asked.

"I know them, I know them!" the candidate said. "Will you please stop worrying? I have a simple technique that will assure victory tonight."

"A simple technique?" the worried manager said. "What is it?"

"I'm going to stick to the facts," the candidate said.

"What? Have you no respect for tradition?"

Humorist Art Buchwald once asked this pertinent question: Have you ever seen a politician talking to a rich person on television?

State Senator Wilbur was seriously considering running for governor, and his aides were busily plugging up any deficiencies that the press might capitalize on during a campaign. Wilbur was dating a woman who sang in a rock band, and his manager was worried about possible trouble. Without disclosing his identity, the manager hired a private detective to do a thorough background check on her.

The report was highly positive. The woman had no scandals in her past, her friends were all respectable people, and her reputation was, in general, excellent. The only possible mark against her was that she'd been known to date a politician with a dubious reputation.

It was election night, and Andrews had his whole family at his campaign headquarters. No one they knew had ever run for political office before, and Andrews stood a good chance of being elected alderman.

When he answered the phone, all talk ceased, and everyone watched Andrews. "Yes," he said. "Yes . . . yes." His face broke into a wide grin. "Thanks!" he said and hung up the phone.

"Listen up, everybody!" he cried. "Especially you, Mom. I've won the election!"

"Honestly?" his mother called out.

"Come on, Mom. This is not the time to bring that up."

"Reverend," said the candidate, "I'm here to ask for your support in my campaign for the state senate."

"Before I make any commitment," the minister said, "let me ask you a question. "Do you partake of alcoholic beverages?"

"Before I answer," the candidate said, "let me ask you a question. Is that an inquiry or an invitation?"

A ten-term congressman was asleep in bed with his wife when she shook him violently and whispered, "Wake up, Arnold! I think there's a thief in the house!"

Without opening his eyes, he muttered, "Impossible. In the Senate, maybe. But never in the House."

One commentator attributed the ups and downs of the economy to the fact that we elect so many yo-yos to Congress.

A successful politician is someone who can give you complete attention without hearing a word you say.

A successful politician is also someone who believes that you don't have to fool all of the people all of the time. During election campaigns is usually enough to do the job.

. . .

Touring an obscure part of his district, a congressman was being led through a factory that specialized in novelty items. He stopped in front of a man who was fashioning what looked like a horse.

"Interesting," the congressman said. "But why is this only the front portion of the body?"

"We build only the front ends," the worker said. "Then we send them to Washington for final assembly."

A tourist climbed out of his car in downtown Washington, D.C. He said to a man standing near the curb, "Listen, I'm going to be only a couple of minutes. Would you watch my car while I run into this store?"

"What?" the man huffed. "Do you realize that I am a member of the United States Senate?"

"Well no," the tourist said, "I didn't realize that. But it's all right. I'll trust you anyway."

Tom, Dick, and Harry, Washington lobbyists all, were discussing the social stratification of the capital. "How can you be sure you've really arrived in this town?" Harry asked.

"You know you've made it," Tom said, "when you're at a party and the president calls to ask your advice on some pending bill."

"No," Dick said. "You know you've made it when the president invites you to the Oval Office to talk with you."

"No, no, no," Harry said. "You know you've made it when you're talking to the president in the Oval Office, the phone rings, the president answers and then says, "It's for you."

• Producers and Directors •

Claude and Clyde, both Hollywood producers, had been best friends for years. Since they hadn't spoken for several days, Claude called Clyde's office.

"Hello?" Clyde said.

"Clyde? This is Claude. How are things?"

"Oh, just great!" Clyde answered. "I've got two

projects working and another one about to come up. I've just signed a long-term contract with Disney, and I bought the rights to a bestseller for only $5,000. How are things with you?"

"I see," Claude said. "I'll call back later when you're alone."

"I'm thrilled to be coming to opening night of your play. Just tell me one thing beforehand—is it a comedy or a tragedy?"

"If we sell out the first four nights, it's a comedy. Anything short of that will be a tragedy."

Herman Manciewicz, who co-wrote *Citizen Kane* with Orson Welles, once said of Welles, "There but for God goes God."

A famous producer approached a teller's window in a bank. "The ATM seems to be broken," he said. "I just want to make this deposit."

The teller smiled at him and said, "I don't know if you remember me, but I was in the musical you produced two years ago. Are you surprised to see me working here?"

"No," the producer said. "I remember hearing you sing.

→ *Was legendary movie producer Samuel Goldwyn really guilty of all those malaproposisms that are regularly attributed to him? We'll probably never know for sure. But here's a small sampling of some of the goofy things Goldwyn was supposed to have said:*

Now, remember, keep what I'm telling you under your belt.

Upon congratulating an employee whose wife had just given birth to a son:
    Goldwyn: So, what did you name him?
    Employee: John.
    Goldwyn: John? How could you name him John? Every Tom, Dick, and Harry is named John.

A verbal contract isn't worth the paper it's printed on.

. . .

Anyone who goes to a psychiatrist needs to have his head examined.

I may not always be right, but I'm never wrong.

■ ■ ■

PART FIVE

Changing the Light Bulb

▲

Where would we be without formula jokes? Think about how much we depend on jokes that begin:

    Knock, knock

or

    What's the difference between . . .

or

    A priest, a minister, and a rabbi are . . .

    Formula jokes like these can be thought of as the lifeblood of the humorist. If you like telling jokes, you've probably been using formulas since you were a mere tyke.

    And now we present a massive collection of one of the most productive formulas of all time—the light bulb joke.

▼

How many psychiatrists does it take to change a light bulb?

One, but the light bulb has to want to change.

How many Microsoft executives does it take to change a light bulb?

None. They simply declare darkness the new standard.

How many narcissists does it take to change a light bulb?

One. He holds the bulb while the world revolves around him.

How many real men does it take to change a light bulb?

None. Real men aren't afraid of the dark.

. . .

How many Ph.D. students does it take to change a light bulb?

One, but it takes ten years.

How many software programmers does it take to change a light bulb?

None. That's a hardware problem.

How many college basketball players does it take to change a light bulb?

The whole team, but they get four credits for doing it.

How many audience members at a matinee does it take to change a light bulb?

Two. One to change it, and one to announce, "Myra, the bulb is being changed."

How many actors does it take to change a light bulb?

Fifteen. One to change it, and 14 to say, "I could have done that."

. . .

How many doctors does it take to change a light bulb?

It depends on how much health insurance the light bulb has.

How many surrealists does it take to change a light bulb?

Two. One to hold the giraffe, and the other to fill the bathtub with brightly colored balloons.

How many mystery writers does it take to change a light bulb?

Two. One to screw the bulb almost all the way in, and the other to give it a surprising twist at the end.

How many Russian leaders does it take to change a light bulb?

Nobody knows. Russian leaders don't last as long as light bulbs.

How many jugglers does it take to change a light bulb?

One, but it takes at least three light bulbs.

. . .

How many politicians does it take to change a light bulb?

Four. One to change it, and the other three to deny that it was ever changed.

How many economists does it take to change a light bulb?

None. If the light bulb needed changing, market forces would have already forced it to happen.

How many social scientists does it take to change a light bulb?

None. Social scientists don't change light bulbs, they search for the root cause of why the light bulb went out.

How many members of Congress does it take to change a light bulb?

Only one, but it has to be a very, very dim bulb.

. . .

How many bureaucrats does it take to change a light bulb?

Two. One to assure us that everything is being done to deal with the problem, and the other to screw a new light bulb into the hot water faucet.

How many anarchists does it take to change a light bulb?

All of them. Or none of them. Or maybe just most of them. We'll have to wait and see what happens.

How many paranoids does it take to change a light bulb?

Who wants to know?

➔ *If you're actually reading this section, instead of just browsing around in it, this would be a good place to take a break. Too many light bulb jokes all at once can have a serious dulling effect on the brain. So go to another section and come back later to finish this one.*

. . .

How many fishermen does it take to change a light bulb?

Five, and you should have seen the size of that light bulb! Five of us were almost not enough!

How many aerospace engineers does it take to change a light bulb?

None. Changing a light bulb isn't rocket science, you know.

How many magazine headline-writers does it take to change a light bulb?

A Vast and Teeming Horde Stretching from Sea to Shining Sea!

How many baby-sitters does it take to change a light bulb?

None. Pampers don't come in a small enough size for light bulbs.

How many pessimists does it take to change a light bulb?

None. The new one won't work any better than the old one did.

. . .

How many optimists does it take to change a light bulb?

None. They know the power will be back on in a minute.

How many circus performers does it take to change a light bulb?

Four. One to change the bulb and three to shout out, "Ta-daaaa!"

How many country music singers does it take to change a light bulb?

Two. One to change it and one to sing about how much she's going to miss the old bulb.

How many feminists does it take to change a light bulb?

THAT ISN'T FUNNY!

How many husbands does it take to change a light bulb?

One, as long as you ask him every day for a month.

. . .

How many visitors to an art gallery does it take to change a light bulb?

Two. One to change it and one to watch and say, "Humph! My four-year-old could have done that!"

How many nuclear physicists does it take to change a light bulb?

Two. One to change the bulb and the other to figure out where to store the old one for the next 10,000 years.

How many gorillas does it take to change a light bulb?

One, but you need many, many light bulbs.

How many lexicographers does it take to change a light bulb?

Two. One to change the bulb and one to point out that he should have changed it to "light bulb."

. . .

How many bad comedians does it take to change a light bulb?

Two. One to change the bulb and one to widen his eyes, grin wildly, and say, "Socket to me!"

■ ■ ■

PART SIX

What I Mean to Say Is . . .

▲

It's time to take a short break from the jokes. No, no, not from the laughs—just from the jokes. We have here a collection of written and spoken bits that don't quite say what they were meant to say. The result is one of the best kinds of humor—the unintentional kind.

▼

→ *It should come as no surprise that politicians are a prime source of this sort of blunder. Most of them pay so little attention to what they're saying that it's a wonder they make any sensible statements at all. Here are a few examples.*

Senator Joseph McCarthy, in response to a report of an attack on his integrity: "That's the most unheard of thing I've ever heard of!"

Candidate George Bush (the elder) on his chances of being elected: "It's no exaggeration to say the undecideds could go either way."

Candidate Dan Quayle on his vision for education: "We're going to have the best educated American people in the world."

. . .

Philadelphia Mayor Frank Rizzo: "The streets are safe in Philadelphia. It's only the people who make them unsafe."

→ *Now that the politicians have you warmed up, consider the hapless headline writers of the world. Their job is to squeeze as much information into as little space as possible. Sometimes they squeeze so hard that they promise an entirely different story from the one that's in front of them.*

See how good you are at deciphering what each of these newspaper headlines was meant to convey. You have our word that every one of them is genuine.

Kids Make Nutritious Snacks

Blame Flies as Talks Deadlock

Clinton Wins Budget Battle; More Lies Ahead

Stolen Painting Found by Tree

Two Teenagers Indicted for Drowning in Lake   .

Marijuana Issue Sent to Joint Committee

James Bond Spat in Court

Police Begin Campaign to Run Down Jaywalkers

Panda Mating Fails; Veterinarian Takes Over

Denver Chapter Will Have Senator for Breakfast

Cops Quiz Victim in Fatal Shooting

Lamb Retiring from USU Animal Department

Mob Torches Police Station, Shops in Indonesia

Lawmakers Back Train Through Iowa

Russia Expels Baptist Minister from Oregon

Jail Releases Upset Judges

Boys and Girls Club Chief out of a Job

Chinese Diver Wins One-Metre Event; Mates on Carpet

Restaurant Loses License for Racism

Bomb Caused Church Bombing

Asphalt Layers Being Stripped in Pa.

City Council to Discuss Nudity in Private

Local High School Dropouts Cut in Half

. . .

Chinese General Donated to Clinton Campaign

Death to Be Explained

Litigant Has No Right to Lay Advisers in Chambers

Council Stands Against Drugs and Biting Dogs

Alcohol Frequently Seen in Cases

President Takes Credit for Drop in Unwed Birth Rate

Shooting Witness Helps Build Murder Case

County Fighting Juice Bar with Dancers

Man Admits Killing Widow to Avoid Facing Death Penalty

Fencing in Swimming Pool Can Save Children's Lives

Nine Arrested for Beating Wrong Man

Man Trying to Get Kite Electrocuted

Crack in Toilet Bowl Leads to Three Arrests

Call for Ban on Toys for Tots Made of Vinyl

Nuns Forgive Break-In, Assault Suspect

Toxic Street Residents Storm out of Public Meeting

Study: Affirmative Action Benefits Broad

Deans Promise to Stop Drinking on Campus

. . .

School Testing Mushrooms

Ex-Nurse Wrongfully Imprisoned Graduates with Law Degree

Tourists Asked to Leave Keys as Florida Prepares for Storm

FBI Adds to Reward for Killing Suspects

Cemetery Allows People to Be Buried by Their Pets

School Board Member Suspected of Honesty

➜ *Typographical errors are always unfortunate, but some—especially in headlines—are more unfortunate than others. These, too, are all real.*

. . .

Experts Suggest Education Standards Might Be
To Lofty

Steamed Pudding and Crap Dip

Please Release Sketch of Suspect in Assault

High School to Colege? It Depends

Man Booked for Wreckless Driving

EMC Cashing in on the Year 200 Glitch

Poll Says 53% Believe Media Offen Make Mis-
takes

Guay Awarded Zonta Club Litaracy Honor

. . .

Survey Finds Many Employees Lacking in Bacic
Skills

Socks Lower in Tokyo

■ ■ ■

PART SEVEN

Quotes and Quips

▲

So much for unintentional humor. Let's get back to the people who actually want us to laugh at what they say and write.

No need for you to go through hundreds of reference books looking for witty quotes on your favorite topics. We've done the culling for you, with an alphabetical list to make your search even easier.

▼

· *Advertising* ·

Doing business without advertising is like winking at a girl in the dark. You know what you're doing, but no one else does.

Stewart H. Britt

Advertising may be described as the science of arresting human intelligence long enough to get money from it.

Stephen Leacock

Few people at the beginning of the 19th century needed an adman to tell them what they wanted.

John Kenneth Galbraith

An advertising agency is 85 percent confusion and 15 percent commission.

Fred Allen

. . .

The person who writes the bank's commercials is not the person who makes the loans.

Anonymous

Early to bed, early to rise, work like hell, and advertise.

Gert Boyle

Half the money I spend on advertising is wasted. The trouble is, I don't know which half.

John Wanamaker

Many a small thing has been made large by the right kind of advertising.

Mark Twain

There is no such thing as bad publicity—except your own obituary.

Brendan Behan

• *Age* •

One of the delights known to age, and beyond the grasp of youth, is that of Not Going.

J.B. Priestley

I think age is a very high price to pay for maturity.

Tom Stoppard

The man who is a pessimist before 48 knows too much; the man who is an optimist after 48 knows too little.

Mark Twain

They tell you you'll lose your mind when you grow older. What they don't tell you is that you won't miss it very much.

Malcolm Cowley

You know you're getting older when the candles cost more than the cake.

Bob Hope

. . .

The older I grow the more I distrust the familiar doctrine that age brings wisdom.

H. L. Mencken

Barbie is 35 years old. Mattel has just introduced her latest accessory—Barbie's ticking biological clock.

Jay Leno

• *Animals* •

Dogs come when they are called. Cats take a message and get back to you.

Mary Bly

I like pigs. Dogs look up to us, cats look down on us, but pigs treat us as equals.

Winston Churchill

Cats are intended to teach us that not everything
in nature has a function.

Garrison Keillor

Animals have these advantages over man: they
have no theologians to instruct them, their funer-
als cost them nothing, and no one starts lawsuits
over their wills.

Voltaire

A dog is the only thing on earth that loves you
more than you love yourself.

Josh Billings

Cats are smarter than dogs. You can't get eight
cats to pull a sled through snow.

Jeff Valdez

• *Art* •

A primitive artist is an amateur whose work sells.

Grandma Moses

. . .

The artistic temperament is a disease that afflicts amateurs.

G. K. Chesterton

People are wrong when they say the opera isn't what it used to be. It is what it used to be. That's what's wrong with it.

Noel Coward

When an opera star sings her head off, she usually improves her appearance.

Victor Borge

Artists can color the sky red because they know it's blue. The rest of us, who aren't artists, must color things the way they really are, or people might think we're stupid.

Jules Feiffer

An amateur is an artist who supports himself with outside jobs, which enable him to paint. A professional is someone whose wife works to enable him to paint.

Ben Shahn

• *Authors and Writing* •

There are no dull subjects. There are only dull writers.

H. L. Mencken

If you can't annoy somebody, there's little point in writing.

Kingsley Amis

Having your book turned into a movie is like seeing your oxen turned into bouillon cubes.

John LeCarre

The trouble with the publishing business is that too many people who have half a mind to write a book do so.

William Targ

. . .

One reason the human race has such a low opinion of itself is that it gets so much of its wisdom from writers.

Wilfred Sheed

As to the Adjective—when in doubt, strike it out.

Mark Twain

There are three rules for writing a novel. Unfortunately, no one knows what they are.

W. Somerset Maugham

It took me 15 years to discover I had no talent for writing, but I couldn't give it up because by that time I was famous.

Robert Benchley

I love being a writer. What I can't stand is the paperwork.

Peter De Vries

Writing is easy. All you do is stare at a blank sheet of paper until drops of blood form on your forehead.

Gene Fowler

. . .

When audiences come to see us authors lecture,
it is largely in the hope that we'll be funnier to
look at than to read.

Sinclair Lewis

Everywhere I go I'm asked if the university stifles
writers. My opinion is that they don't stifle
enough of them. There's many a bestseller that
could have been prevented by a good teacher.

Flannery O'Connor

Teaching has ruined more American novelists
than drink.

Gore Vidal

If writers were good businessmen, they'd have
too much sense to be writers.

Irwin S. Cobb

• *Beauty* •

I'm tired of all this nonsense about beauty being only skin-deep. That's deep enough. What do you want, an adorable pancreas?

Jean Kerr

It's a good thing that beauty is only skin-deep, or I'd be rotten to the core.

Phyllis Diller

The body of a young woman is God's greatest achievement. Of course, he could have made it last longer.

Neil Simon

Any girl can be glamorous. All you have to do is stand still and look stupid.

Hedy Lamarr

My face looks like a wedding cake left out in the rain.

W. H. Auden

. . .

Sunburn is very becoming, but only when it is even. One must be careful not to look like a mixed grill.

Noel Coward

Her features did not seem to know the value of teamwork.

George Ade

If, after I depart this vale, you ever remember me and have thought to please my ghost, forgive some sinner and wink at some homely girl.

H. L. Mencken

You think beautiful girls are going to stay in style forever?

Barbra Streisand

Had Cleopatra's nose been shorter, the whole history of the world would have been different.

Blaise Pascal

◆ *Business* ◆

When you become a businessman you become stagnant in some ways. You don't do as many of the exciting and dangerous things you used to do. It was either skydiving or [the New York Yankees].

George Steinbrenner

Business is a good game—lots of competition and a minimum of rules. You keep score with money.
Nolan Bushnell

Almost everything I have is for sale, except my kids and possibly my wife.

Carl Icahn

I come from an environment where, if you see a snake, you kill it. At GM, if you see a snake, the first thing you do is go hire a consultant on snakes.

Ross Perot

. . .

The salary of the chief executive of the large corporation is not a market award for achievement. It is frequently in the nature of a warm personal gesture by the individual to himself.

John Kenneth Galbraith

It takes five years to develop a new car in this country. Heck, we won World War II in four years.

Ross Perot

There are two times in a man's life when he should not speculate: when he can't afford it, and when he can.

Mark Twain

My father always told me that all businessmen are sons of bitches, but I never believed it until now.

John F. Kennedy

I find it rather easy to portray a businessman. Being bland, rather cruel, and incompetent comes naturally to me.

John Cleese

Under capitalism, man exploits man. Under socialism, the reverse is true.

Polish Proverb

• *Children* •

I love children, especially when they cry, for then someone takes them away.

Nancy Mitford

Reasoning with a child is fine, if you can reach the child's reason without destroying your own.

John Mason Brown

The best way to keep children at home is to make the home atmosphere pleasant—and let the air out of the tires.

Dorothy Parker

The reason grandparents and children get along so well is that they have a common enemy.

Sam Levenson

. . .

A critic is a man created to praise greater men than himself, but he is never able to find them.
Richard La Gallienne

A critic is a man who knows the way but can't drive the car.
Kenneth Tynan

What the critics said hurt me very much. I cried all the way to the bank.
Liberace

Nature fits all her children with something to do;
He who would write and can't can surely review.
James Russell Lowell

When a book and a head come into co
one of them sounds hollow, is it alway
Arthur

. . .

Before I got married I had six theories about bringing up children. Now I have six children and no theories.
Lord Rochester

I could now afford all the things I didn't have as a kid, if I didn't have kids.
Robert Orben

Anyone who hates children and dogs can't be all bad.
Norman Rosten
(referring to W. C. Fields)

The young always have the same problem—how to rebel and conform at the same time. They have now solved this by defying their parents and copying one another.
Quentin Crisp

• *Clothes* •

You can say what you want about long dresses,
but they cover a multitude of shins.

Mae West

Distrust any enterprise that requires new clothes.

Henry David Thoreau

She wears her clothes as if they had been thrown
on her with a pitchfork.

Jonathan Swift

You'd be surprised how much it costs to look this
cheap.

Dolly Parton

What would we say if men changed the length of
their trousers every year?

Lady Astor

. . .

High heels were invented by a woman who ha
been kissed on the forehead.

Christopher M

• *Critics* •

Critics are like eunuchs in a harem. They kno
how it's done, they've seen it done every day,
they're unable to do it themselves.

Brendan E

A critic is a gong at a railroad crossing clangi
loudly and vainly as the train goes by.

Christopher M

Critics are like pigs at the pastry cart.

John U

. . .

Reviewing has one advantage over suicide. In suicide you take it out on yourself; in reviewing you take it out on other people.

George Bernard Shaw

• *Death* •

Death is the greatest kick of all. That's why they save it till last.

Anonymous

Most people would rather die than think; in fact, they do so.

Bertrand Russell

For three days after death, hair and fingernails continue to grow. But phone calls taper off.

Johnny Carson

. . .

Those who welcome death have only tried it from the ears up.

Wilson Mizner

It's not that I'm afraid of death. I just don't want to be there when it happens.

Woody Allen

◆ *Eating and Drinking* ◆

A gourmet who thinks of calories is like a tart who looks at her watch.

James Beard

Once during Prohibition I was forced to live for days on nothing but food and water.

W. C. Fields

. . .

The egg cream is psychologically the opposite of circumcision. It pleasurably reaffirms your Jewishness.

Mel Brooks

I don't like spinach, and I'm glad I don't, because if I liked it I'd eat it, and I'd just hate it.

Clarence Darrow

Cheese is milk's leap toward immortality.

Clifton Fadiman

Great food is like great sex. The more you have, the more you want.

Gail Greene

A prohibitionist is a man one wouldn't care to drink with, even if he drank.

H. L. Mencken

A fruit is a vegetable with money. Plus, if you let it rot, it turns into wine, something Brussels sprouts never do.

P. J. O'Rourke

Never eat more than you can lift.

Miss Piggy

I have never been drunk, but I have often been overserved.

George Gobel

I will not eat oysters. I want my food dead—not sick, not wounded—dead.

Woody Allen

One more drink and I'd have been under the host.

Dorothy Parker

Large, naked raw carrots are acceptable as food only to those who live in hutches, eagerly awaiting Easter.

Fran Lebowitz

. . .

One reason I don't drink is that I want to know
when I'm having a good time.

Nancy Astor

A cucumber should be well sliced and dressed
with pepper and vinegar, and then thrown out as
good for nothing.

Samuel Johnson

An alcoholic is a man you don't like who drinks as
much as you do.

Dylan Thomas

• *Education* •

If you think education is expensive, try ignorance.

Derek Bok

I have never let my schooling interfere with my
education.

Mark Twain

. . .

Spoon-feeding in the long run teaches us nothing
but the shape of the spoon.

E. M. Forster

Society produces rogues, and education makes
one rogue cleverer than another.

Oscar Wilde

Education is the inculcation of the incomprehensi-
ble into the indifferent by the incompetent.

John Maynard Keynes

You can always tell a Harvard man—but you can't
tell him much.

Elbert Hubbard

Training is everything. The peach was once a bitter almond; cauliflower is nothing but cabbage
with a college education.

Mark Twain

. . .

Soap and education are not as sudden as a massacre, but they are more deadly in the long run.
Mark Twain

A good education enables you to earn more than a good educator.

Anonymous

A man who has never been to school may steal from a freight car. But if he has a university education, he may steal the whole railroad.
Theodore Roosevelt

A learned blockhead is a greater blockhead than an ignorant one.

Benjamin Franklin

• *Fame* •

A celebrity is a person who works all his life to become known, then wears dark glasses to avoid being recognized.

Fred Allen

Now when I bore people at parties, they think it's their fault.

Henry Kissinger

Fame is a vapor, popularity an accident. The only earthly certainty is oblivion.

Mark Twain

Men often mistake notoriety for fame and would rather be remembered for their vices and follies than not be noticed at all.

Harry Truman

If I had done everything I'm credited with, I'd be speaking to you from a laboratory jar at Harvard.

Frank Sinatra

Being a star has made it possible for me to get insulted in places where the average Negro could never hope to get insulted.

Sammy Davis, Jr.

A sign of a celebrity is that his name is often worth more than his services.

Daniel Boorstein

It took [Phil Silvers] 20 years to become an overnight sensation.

Milton Berle

◆ *Friends and Enemies* ◆

When you are down and out, something always turns up—and it is usually the noses of your friends.

Orson Welles

. . .

A true friend is one who likes you despite your achievements.

Arnold Bennett

No one is completely unhappy at the failure of his best friend.

Groucho Marx

It is difficult to say who do you the most mis-chief—enemies with the worst intentions or friends with the best.

Edward Bulwer-Lytton

Friends are God's apology for relations.

Hugh Kingsmill

I ask you to judge me by the enemies I have made.

Franklin D. Roosevelt

The one thing your friends will never forgive you is your happiness.

Albert Camus

. . .

Money can't buy friends, but you get a better
class of enemy.

Spike Milligan

There are three faithful friends—an old wife, an
old dog, and ready money.

Benjamin Franklin

Forgive your enemies, but never forget their
names.

John F. Kennedy

It takes your enemy and your friend, working together, to hurt you—the one to slander you, and
the other to bring the news to you.

Mark Twain

• *Government* •

There's no trick to being a humorist when you
have the whole government working for you.

Will Rogers

. . .

The only thing that saves us from the bureaucracy is its inefficiency.

Eugene McCarthy

Blessed are the young, for they shall inherit the
national debt.

Herbert Hoover

A government is the only known vessel that leaks
from the top.

James Reston

If the opposite of *pro* is *con,* then what is the opposite of *progress?*

Anonymous

Society is produced by our wants, and government by our wickedness.

Thomas Paine

. . .

In general, the art of government consists in taking as much money as possible from one class of
the citizens to give it to the other.

Voltaire

Reader, suppose you were an idiot; and suppose
you were a member of Congress—but I repeat
myself.

Mark Twain

When I was a boy, I was told that anybody could
become president. I'm beginning to believe it.

Clarence Darrow

⋅ *Happiness* ⋅

Happiness is not something you experience. It's
something you remember.

Oscar Levant

. . .

Happiness *n.* An agreeable sensation arising from contemplating the misery of another.

Ambrose Bierce

Some cause happiness wherever they go; others whenever they go.

Oscar Wilde

Happiness is having a large, loving, caring, close-knit family—in another city.

George Burns

It's a good thing God doesn't let you look into the future, or you might be sorely tempted to shoot yourself.

Lee Iacocca

It isn't necessary to be rich and famous to be happy. It's only necessary to be rich.

Alan Alda

. . .

Happiness makes up in height for what it lacks in length.

Robert Frost

Happiness is good health and a bad memory.

Ingrid Bergman

◆ *Humility* ◆

Humility is no substitute for a good personality.

Fran Lebowitz

If only I had a little humility, I would be perfect.

Ted Turner

• *Laughter* •

He who laughs has not yet heard the bad news.
Bertolt Brecht

You grow up the day you have your first real
laugh—at yourself.

Ethel Barrymore

The penalty for laughing in a court of law is six
months in jail. If it were not for this penalty, the
jury would never hear the evidence.

H. L. Mencken

The world is so overflowing with absurdity that it
is difficult for the humorist to compete.

Malcolm Muggeridge

I remain one thing and one thing only, and that is
a clown. It places me on a far higher plane than
any politician.

Charlie Chaplin

• *Law and Lawyers* •

If law school is so tough to get through, how come there are so many lawyers?

Calvin Trillin

Law school is the opposite of sex. Even when it's good, it's lousy.

Anonymous

I have knowingly defended a number of guilty men. But the guilty never escape unscathed. My fees are sufficient punishment for anyone.

F. Lee Bailey

Lawyers, I suppose, were children once.

Charles Lamb

It is better to have loved and lost, but only if you have a good lawyer.

Herb Caen

. . .

When you go into court, you're putting your fate
into the hands of 12 people who weren't smart
enough to get out of jury duty.

Norm Crosby

A judge is a law student who marks his own examination papers.

H. L. Mencken

A judge is a lawyer who once knew a politician.

Anonymous

• *Love* •

Love *n.* A temporary insanity curable by marriage.

Ambrose Bierce

If you want to read about love and marriage,
you've got to buy two separate books.

Alan King

. . .

By the time you swear you're his,
  Shivering and sighing,
  And he vows his passion is
  Infinite, undying—
  One of you is lying.

Dorothy Parker

Men always want to be a woman's first love.
Women have a more subtle instinct—what they
like is to be a man's last romance.

Oscar Wilde

Love consists of overestimating the difference between one woman and another.

George Bernard Shaw

Love is the word used to label the sexual excite-
ment of the young, the habituation of the middle-
aged, and the mutual dependence of the old.

John Ciardi

. . .

Love is said to be blind, but I know a lot of fellows in love who can see twice as much in their sweethearts as I can.

Josh Billings

A woman drove me to drink, and I never even had the courtesy to thank her.

W. C. Fields

Love conquers all things—except poverty and toothache.

Mae West

Love is only a dirty trick played on us to achieve the continuation of the species.

W. Somerset Maugham

• *Marriage* •

Marriage *n*. The state or condition of a community consisting of a master, a mistress, and two slaves, making two in all.

Ambrose Bierce

. . .

The only real argument for marriage is that it remains the best method for getting acquainted.
Heywood Broun

It wasn't actually a divorce. I was traded.
Tim Conway

Basically, my wife is immature. I'd be at home in the bath and she'd come in and sink my boats.
Woody Allen

My son got his first acting part, playing a man who's been married for 30 years. I told him to stick at it, and next time he'd get a speaking part.
Henry Fonda

Only two things are necessary to keep one's wife happy. One is to let her think she's having her own way; the other is to let her have it.
Lyndon Baines Johnson

. . .

It was good of God to let [Thomas] Carlyle and Mrs. Carlyle marry one another and so make only two people miserable instead of four.

Samuel Butler

• *Military* •

Military justice is to justice what military music is to music.

Georges Clemenceau

Military intelligence is a contradiction in terms.

Groucho Marx

Being in the army is like being in the Boy Scouts, except that the Boy Scouts have adult supervision.

Blake Clark

Join the army, see the world, meet interesting people—and kill them.

Woody Allen

• *Money* •

My favorite dish is mixed greens: twenties, fifties, and hundreds.

Eileen Mason

The rich are different from you and me because they have more credit.

John Leonard

For the *Wall Street Journal* to criticize my wife for making money is like *Field and Stream* criticizing someone for catching a fish.

Bill Clinton

There is nothing so habit-forming as money.

Don Marquis

I'm living so far beyond my income that we may almost be said to be living apart.

e e cummings

I made my money the right way. My grandfather gave it to me.

Rep. Joseph Kennedy

. . .

Lack of money is the root of all evil.
George Bernard Shaw

When a fellow says, "It ain't the money, but the principle of the thing," it's the money.
Elbert Hubbard

I'm tired of hearing about money, money, money. I just want to play the game—and drink Pepsi and wear Reebok.
Shaquille O'Neal

• *Politics* •

The difference between horse racing and politics is that in horse racing the whole horse wins.
Anonymous

I guess I should warn you, if I turn out to be particularly clear, you've probably misunderstood what I've said.
Alan Greenspan

. . .

A politician is an animal which can sit on a fence
and yet keep both ears to the ground.

H. L. Mencken

Being president is like running a cemetery.
You've got a lot of people under you, but none of
them are listening.

Bill Clinton

The difference between being an elder statesman
and posing as an elder statesman is practically
negligible.

T. S. Eliot

Liberals feel unworthy of their possessions. Con-
servatives feel they deserve everything they've
stolen.

Mort Sahl

• *Procrastination* •

Procrastination is the art of keeping up with yesterday.

Don Marquis

Work is the greatest thing in the world, so we should always save some of it for tomorrow.

Don Herold

Never put off till tomorrow what you can do the day after tomorrow.

Mark Twain

• *Puritanism* •

Puritanism: The haunting fear that someone, somewhere may be happy.

H. L. Mencken

. . .

The Puritan hated bear-baiting not because it
gave pain to the bear, but because it gave pleasure
to the spectators.

Thomas B. Macaulay

• *Religion* •

Imagine the Creator as a low comedian, and at
once the world becomes explicable.

H. L. Mencken

We have just enough religion to make us hate, but
not enough to make us love one another.

Jonathan Swift

I'm a born-again atheist.

Gore Vidal

I admire the serene assurance of those who have
religious faith. It is wonderful to observe the calm
confidence of a Christian with four aces.

Mark Twain

. . .

Most religions do not make men better, only
warier.

Elias Canetti

• *Sex* •

If your sexual fantasies were truly of interest to
others, they would no longer be fantasies.

Fran Lebowitz

In my sex fantasy, nobody ever loves me for my
mind.

Nora Ephron

It has to be admitted that we English have sex on
the brain, which is a very unsatisfactory place to
have it.

Malcolm Muggeridge

. . .

Love is the answer. But while you're waiting for
the answer, sex raises some pretty good questions.

Woody Allen

Chastity is the most unnatural of the sexual per-
versions.

Aldous Huxley

Sex is the thing that takes up the least amount of
time and causes the most amount of trouble.

John Barrymore

The pleasure is momentary, the position ridiculous, and the expense damnable.

Lord Chesterfield

If sex is such a natural phenomenon, how come
there are so many books on "how to"?

Bette Midler

• *Show Business* •

I do not want actors and actresses to understand my plays. That is not necessary. If they will only pronounce the correct sounds, I can guarantee the results.

George Bernard Shaw

You can take all the sincerity in Hollywood, place it in the navel of a fruit fly, and still have room enough for three caraway seeds and a producer's heart.

Fred Allen

Strip away the phony tinsel of Hollywood and you find the real tinsel underneath.

Oscar Levant

Hollywood is a place where people from Iowa mistake each other for movie stars.

Fred Allen

. . .

Acting is not an important job in the scheme of things. Plumbing is.

Spencer Tracy

Actors spend their lives doing something they put people in asylums for.

Jane Fonda

• *Sports* •

Football bears the same relationship to education that bullfighting bears to ranching.

Elbert Hubbard

Football combines the two worst features of American life. It is violence punctuated by committee meetings.

George F. Will

. . .

When a man wants to murder a tiger, he calls it sport. When a tiger wants to murder him, he calls it ferocity.

George Bernard Shaw

Skiing? I do not participate in any sport with ambulances at the bottom of the hill.

Erma Bombeck

Fishermen and hypochondriacs have one thing in common. They don't have to catch anything to be happy.

Robert Orben

The fascination of shooting as a sport depends almost wholly on whether you are at the right or wrong end of the gun.

P. G. Wodehouse

A puck is a hard rubber disk that hockey players strike when they can't hit each other.

Jimmy Cannon

. . .

Give me my golf clubs, fresh air, and a beautiful partner, and you can keep the golf clubs and the fresh air.

Jack Benny

Playing polo is like trying to play golf during an earthquake.

Sylvester Stallone

Golf is a good walk spoiled.

Mark Twain

It has always been my private conviction that any man who pits his intelligence against a fish and loses has it coming.

John Steinbeck

• *Success* •

I have often thought it might very well appear . . . on my tombstone . . . , "Here lies Paul Newman, who died a complete failure because his eyes suddenly turned brown."

Paul Newman

The trick is to make sure you don't die before prosperity comes.

Lee Iacocca

Be awful nice to 'em goin' up, because you're gonna meet 'em all comin' down.

Jimmy Durante

Maybe I should drop dead. It would be a good career move. Look what it did for Glenn Miller.

Band leader Artie Shaw

A full moon blanks out all the stars around it.

Ted Turner
about himself

It is better to be approximately right than precisely wrong.

Warren Buffett

So many people have claimed to be the father of
the Mustang that I wouldn't want to be seen in
public with the mother.

Lee Iacocca

[Euro Disney has] already had a million Germans
and a million British guests, and to have those
numbers in France without a war going on is really something.

Michael Eisner

◆ *Television* ◆

Television is chewing gum for the eyes.

Fred Allen

Television is for appearing on—not for looking at.

Noel Coward

My father hated radio and could not wait for television to be invented so he could hate that too.

Peter De Vries

. . .

Television is a medium of entertainment which
permits millions of people to listen to the same
joke at the same time and yet remain lonesome.

T. S. Eliot

Television is an invention that permits you to be
entertained in your living room by people you
wouldn't have in your home.

David Frost

Television has proved that people will look at anything rather than each other.

Ann Landers

Imitation is the sincerest form of television.

Fred Allen

Television is called a medium because it is neither
rare nor well done.

Ernie Kovacs

• *Virtue and Vice* •

The Golden Rule is that there are no golden rules.
George Bernard Shaw

My only aversion to vice—is the price.
Victor Buono

It has been my experience that folks who have no vices have very few virtues.
Abraham Lincoln

One big vice in a man is apt to keep out a great many smaller ones.
Bret Harte

He hasn't a single redeeming vice.
Oscar Wilde

Most people want to be delivered from temptation but would like it to keep in touch.
Robert Orben

. . .

Woman's virtue is man's greatest invention.
Cornelia Otis Skinner

• *Work* •

It is impossible to enjoy idling thoroughly unless one has plenty of work to do.
Jerome K. Jerome

My son is now an entrepreneur. That's what you're called when you don't have a job.
Ted Turner

The reason why worry kills more people than work is that more people worry than work.
Robert Frost

Never buy anything with a handle on it. It means work.
H. Allen Smith

. . .

Every morning I get up and look through the
Forbes list of the richest people in America. If I'm
not there, I go to work.

Robert Orben

One machine can do the work of 50 ordinary
men. No machine can do the work of 1 extraordi-
nary man.

Elbert Hubbard

■ ■ ■

PART EIGHT

Make 'Em Laugh

▲

What's the biggest challenge in putting together a joke book? Just as it is with a joke, delivering a good ending is the hard part. We've decided to end this book with a handful of jokes that constitute a classification all their own. One good thing about these jokes is that they're the kind that just about anyone can make up. But more about that later. Let's start with a sample.

▼

A frog walks into a bank and sits at the desk of one of the loan officers, a Ms. Patricia Wack. "Good morning, Patty," the frog says, annoying her right off the bat. "I want to borrow $5,000."

"I see," says Ms. Wack, trying very hard not to lose her composure. "And do you have any collateral?"

"Not a thing," says the frog.

"In that case," Ms. Wack says, "I'll have to check your credit rating."

"Don't bother, Patty," the frog says. "I don't have any credit rating."

"Well," Ms. Wack says, "with no credit rating and no collateral, I'm afraid you can't expect us to lend you any money."

"Tell you what, Patty," the frog says, "you do whatever you have to do to get me the $5,000 loan, and I'll give you $500 of it off the top. No strings attached."

Flustered, Ms. Wack says she has to talk to her supervisor. She repeats the whole conversation to him. Then she says, "I don't understand this business about the $500."

Her boss looks at her, smiles, and says, "It's a kickback, Patty Wack. Give the frog a loan."

→ *Yes, it's true that, in order for that joke to work, your listeners have to be familiar with the repeated line from the children's song "This Old Man." If it turns out that they aren't, you'll just have to smile bravely and move on into the next room. The odds, however, are in your favor. Here's another, this one based on the name of a very well known household product.*

When the driver of a huge trailer lost control of his rig, he plowed into an empty tollbooth and smashed it to pieces. He climbed down from the wreckage and within a matter of minutes, a truck pulled up and discharged a crew of workers.

The men picked up each broken piece of the former tollbooth and spread some kind of creamy substance on it. Then they began fitting the pieces together. In less than a half hour, they had the entire tollbooth reconstructed and looking as good as new.

"Astounding!" the truck driver said to the crew chief. "What was that white stuff you used to get all those pieces together?"

The crew chief said, "Oh, that was tollgate booth paste."

The waiter at the Dew Drop Inn had just finished putting up the Christmas decorations when the first customer of the evening came in.

"Why, Tom Barclay," the waiter exclaimed, "I haven't seen you in years. Home for Christmas?"

"That's right," Barclay said. "And I couldn't come back home without stopping in for those famous eggs benedict of yours."

"Coming right up," the waiter said.

Barclay took a seat, and ten minutes later the waiter returned, carrying the eggs benedict on a silver hubcap.

Puzzled, Barclay asked, "What's the idea of the hubcap?"

In response, the waiter sang, "Oh, there's no plate like chrome for the hollandaise!"

→ *Don't try the next one on anyone who hasn't taken some classes in basic geometry. Also, do your best to avoid the kind of informed person*

who might question how a Native American
tribe would have managed to slay a hippopota-
mus.

In a certain Indian tribe 200 years ago, the
squaws of the chiefs often displayed their belong-
ings to show who was more important. In one
tent, three squaws sat on animal hides. One sat on
the hide of a deer, a second on the hide of a
moose, and a third on the hide of a hippo. The
first two squaws displayed an impressive amount
of worldly goods. The one on the hide of the
hippo, however, displayed the same amount of
goods herself as the other two combined.

In other words, the squaw on the hippopotamus
was equal to the sum of the squaws on the other
two hides.

➔ *Now for a couple of examples that might be*
called classics, if such a word could be used for
the kind of terrible, far-fetched puns that these
jokes rely on. For these, we have to go back
into the previous millennium.

Some of your listeners might need to be re-
minded of a song that was wildly popular

around the middle of the 20th century, a song about taking a train ride out of Tennessee. The opening line of the song is, "Pardon me, boy, is that the Chattanooga Choo-Choo?" Thirty or so years later, a brief fad made that line the basis of dozens of jokes like these two.

Singer Roy Orbison left his hotel room for Madison Square Garden, an hour before what promised to be his biggest show of the year. He'd had a nice meal and a good rest, and he was ready for the concert that would be the basis of a TV special.

When he reached his dressing room, however, he saw a sight that threatened to ruin the whole evening. He'd bought a new pair of boots for this concert, and there they were on the floor, torn and shredded, as though they'd been attacked by an animal.

It turned out to be an animal. His staff reminded him that a magazine writer who had interviewed him earlier in the day had carried a Siamese cat with her. While Roy was having dinner, she'd left the cat in the room unattended.

The staff was deployed to several stores around Madison Square Garden, and they came back with four pairs of boots. Orbison wasn't thrilled to be replacing his custom-mades, but one of the pairs fit pretty well, and he decided he could go on after all.

On his way out to the stage, one of his aides spotted the woman and her cat. He turned to his boss and said, "Pardon me, Roy, is that the cat who chewed your new shoes?"

The grand prize on the British TV game show *Pick the Winner* was a trip around the world. The challenge was to decide which of three contestants was telling the truth about some incident in his or her private life.

Montgomery listened carefully, watched the facial expressions and body language of all three speakers, and finally opted for Speaker No. 3. The host screamed that Montgomery had chosen correctly.

Backstage after the show, Montgomery was introduced to Speaker No. 3, Mrs. Joy Welles. After they'd spoken for a few minutes, Mr. Welles arrived to drive his wife home.

Before Mrs. Welles could introduce her husband to Montgomery, Mr. Welles said, "Pardon me, Joy, is this the chap who knew to choose you?"

. . .

→ *We said something earlier about making up jokes like these. It isn't nearly as difficult as you might expect, but you do need a powerful tolerance for outrageous puns. Just start with some well-known phrase or sentence—a song title, a catch phrase from this year's hot comedy movie, a famous quotation. Then play around with it until you've twisted it into a series of awful puns. Finally—and this is usually the fun part—make up some ridiculously far-fetched story to justify the pun. The longer the story you invent, the louder will be the groans (of appreciation, you should remind yourself) from your listeners.*

We'll bow out with a few more of these jokes, just to get you thinking along the right lines.

There was a terrible fire at a Basque movie theater in Spain. In violation of all regulations, there was only one useable exit, and several people were unable to get out of the theater.

When will people learn that you shouldn't put all your Basques in one exit?

. . .

Horace Silas was a determined inventor in the 19th century, but everything he came up with ended up by the wayside. Finally, after years of producing gadgets no one had any use for, Silas had a brainstorm that would make thousands of bakers happy.

He invented a series of double-bladed knives that could slice two loaves at a time into a dozen slices. He patented the invention and made a nice little bundle on it.

Seeing the possibilities, Silas tinkered with his invention until he could slice three loaves at a time. But he wasn't satisfied until he managed to extend its capabilities to four loaves at once.

With this last invention, Silas became the inventor of the four-loaf cleaver.

Two boll weevils grew up together in Alabama. One of them decided to go out into the world and make his fortune. He went north, got into the fabric business, and won fame and fortune.

The other one stayed in Alabama and was completely unknown outside his home county. He became known as the lesser of two weevils.

NASA's latest goal is to study the effects of space travel on various kinds of animals we use for food.

The first experiment will involve sending several cows and bulls up in a spaceship.

They will refer to it as the herd shot round the world.

A scientific expedition returned from the South Pacific with several pieces of news. One involved the discovery of a palm frond that could be ground into suppositories to treat constipation.

During a press conference, the leader of the scientific team was asked if these palm fronds really were better than existing treatments.

"Are you kidding?" the scientist replied. "With fronds like these, who needs enemas?"

A swami from India told his dentist not to use Novocaine during drilling. When the doctor objected, the swami explained, "I want to transcend dental medication."

The hotel was sponsoring a national chess tournament, and the manager was pretty fed up with the whole affair. He'd had complaints from the help about the paucity of tips, the players tended to be obnoxious at every opportunity, and the chambermaids kept finding these little pawns in the most unlikely places throughout the rooms.

Now the manager was quietly steaming while six chess players monopolized the lobby with boisterous rantings about their recent victories. After several guests complained, he approached the group.

"Enough," he announced. "I want you people out of the lobby."

"And just why would we have to leave?" one of them asked.

"Because," the manager said, "I can't stand chess nuts boasting in an open foyer."

Index